THE
NEW AGE
Handbook On
DEATH
and
DYING

BY
Carol W. Parrish-Harra

IBS Press
Santa Monica, California

Dedicated to
MARY BETH, ALEXIS
and all the others

Contents

Preface

While reading this book, I kept wishing that there were many more people like the author! It is written with such a rare, tender and thorough perception of all that human beings go through, that it is bound to be a comfort and inspiration which is much needed in the world today.

This period in history is producing such intensive suffering, bereavement, homelessness and unemployment all over the world, that only the most inspired, fundamental and vigorous help will be of any consequence. Carol Parrish-Harra's spiritual background enables her to write from experience. One even feels that she could, if she would, say much more regarding the hidden causes behind the apparently unreasonable sufferings which are the lot of many who do not seem to merit them in any way. Instead, she remains in the realm of practical, understandable spiritualism. She realizes with great wisdom, the value of being *natural,* of weeping at need, of accepting personal comfort from others, as well as giving it; and of avoiding, above all, the danger of repression with its long aftermaths.

There is something for everyone in this encyclopedia of dying. Christ spoke about our "second birth," which I feel refers to the birth of the soul *within* the body, when the human aspiration makes it possible. This book deals with the "third birth," when the individual, having passed through the essential *school* of physical life, is reborn with acquired maturity into the expansive wonder of the inner worlds — surely a moment of intense rejoicing.

Vera Stanley Alder
Bournemouth, England

Foreword

Each death is a poignant love story. Each drama is unique and special, just as each birth. We dare not avoid these powerful experiences because *death is life too*.

In the past five years I have been sharing with a few people some stories of great value to me. These stories are real. They are dynamic in their impact on me and my picture of life. This book is my personal conversation with you about them.

A part of my ministry is devoted to assisting people to heal and to hope, even in the face of death. This type of healing rests on the belief that just as there is a natural time to be born, there is a correct time for us to die; a proper moment to let go of life as we know it and to begin anew at some other stage.

In recent years, significant research has seemed to reinforce the idea of continuity of life. Old ideas are being presented in the context of the newly researched experiences of those who have been resuscitated and revived, and a fresh picture is coming into focus. A new vista is opening that will facilitate better understanding of spiritual teachings and inspired writing concerned with death, giving help and hope to many who are not certain what to believe.

I have experienced many kinds of death in life — the death of hopes, prejudices and relationships, as well as the physical deaths of loved ones. But my near-death experience when I was in my twenties totally assured me there is more to life than we readily acknowledge. Later experiences confirmed this.

As a counselor, I use the material in this book to prepare persons for their own death experience. I offer people methods which encourage open expression of fear and unrestrained questioning, so that some comfort can enter into their lives at this delicate and special time. In addition, I make suggestions for the construction of a precious and close-knit support system for each participant during the final period of time. This unity is most beneficial for the survivors as well as the one passing. I write only from my own experience, about proven techniques for expanding limited and painful views of death. I believe these insights will provide you with comfort and a stronger belief in a living Creator with a perfect plan.

Carol W. Parrish-Harra

Introduction

Insight into the Greatest
Experience of All

Since the original publication of this book, Carol Parrish-Harra has continued her explorations into the near-death experience, and her pioneering work with the dying has drawn world-wide attention. In the following interview, Carol Parrish-Harra discusses her views on death and dying with John White, a noted author and lecturer in the fields of consciousness research and human development.

A New Age Approach to Death and Dying: Insight Into the Greatest Experience of All, by John White, copyright November, 1987 by *Science of Mind* magazine, is reprinted here with permission of *Science of Mind* magazine.

JW: *You describe your ministry as devoted to assisting people to heal and to hope, even in the face of death, and a major part of your ministry is working with the dying and their families. Would you elaborate on that? How can death be a healing?*

CPH: I feel the dying experience is an opportunity to heal relationships and the stress of a person's life. When we know we're going to die, we can consciously evaluate our life and see for ourselves — especially if we're talking and sharing with others — our unfinished business. We can seek to mend broken relationships. If we want to understand ourselves — why we did certain things, what was the result of certain steps we took — counselors can give us feedback and help us explore ourselves. I particularly try to help people see the positive result of their efforts in life. I try to get them to share what they have in common with other family members, almost like an inheritance. If the dying don't do that, children and grandchildren are at a loss. If they *do* share, then after the father, mother, or whomever has passed on, that sharing becomes a real treasure of the family.

I look for what can be drawn out of a situation that will live long afterward, such as the stories that the one passing on leaves as an inheritance for the family. To do that, though, one usually has to get the relationship with the family into a good place. Sometimes it already is, sometimes it isn't. Nearly always there are some areas where it hasn't all been done, and there's some member of the family who feels left out or has no communication. So some effort must be made to bring that person back in touch with the one who's passing on.

JW: *Is this emphasis on healing relationships what you mean by a New Age approach? How does the New Age perspective on death and dying differ from the old one?*

CPH: I feel the New Age aspect which differs most involves being able to talk about death and consciously prepare for it. I think the New Age counselor must help dying people explore what they think they're going to experience in death — not taking a dogmatic approach but simply encouraging them to articulate for themselves what *they* think is going to happen, looking at what they feel about death and how they have arrived at that perspective. Also I often talk about the near-death experience because I happen to have had such an experience. That can help them think about the afterlife or spiritual world. People don't have to accept any of what I say, of course, and I don't feel I'm supposed to convince them of anything. I'm just trying to comfort them and help them open up to think about ongoing life in a different way.

JW: *The death process can be divided into three aspects. There's the time of dying, which may be brief or long. Then there's the transitional moment into death itself. Last is postmortem existence. What is your perspective with regard to the moment of transition and postmortem experience?*

CPH: I use my personal experience, including my near-death, as part of my picture describing the moment of death and transition. I tell people that I feel assurance within myself there is a Love, an Intelligence, an all-knowing state, that is positive. What makes it hard for humanity is that a veil hides that Love-Intelligence. It's as though we operate on one side of the veil, not knowing what's on the other side and afraid to go beyond it. So talking about my near-death experience or sharing that I encountered great compassion, love, and richness in the experience reassures or brings hope to a person that he or she is going toward something good — something good beyond comprehension, not toward a fate that is judgmental or unkind; not to hell-fire or damnation.

That has been an important part of my work with people as they were dying. I have not presumed that I knew what the afterlife as such will be. I simply suggest things to people and let them find out for themselves, ultimately. I like to introduce people to written material. I like to introduce them to the concept of reincarnation. I don't feel I have to convert them to my point of view. I merely suggest that in the sacred writings of the various traditions there's enough said about the afterlife and the after-world to give a clear picture about the ongoing nature of the process. I even talk about apparitions and reappearances of lost family members. Oftentimes families have their own stories of when someone came in and saw a certain deceased relative in the room. In its simplest form, it at least makes the dying person think, "That couldn't have happened if there isn't some form of afterlife to be dealt with." So I feel my first job is to encourage the dying to think there is an afterlife. If they have not thought this through on their own, if it's not an integrated part of them, then I try to get them to accept it and integrate it and help it to become their own reality.

JW: *Is it important for a person to have a particular belief system?*

CPH: I don't think a person's philosophy or belief system is as important as their somehow finding a way to feel identified with the ongoing big part of life. For example, say a person is working to mend a relationship with someone he's leaving behind. The person might say, "I don't see how this is going to make my death any easier."

And I'll say, "No, it may not. But talking about it may help the other person. Try to look at it from that perspective." Suppose the other person is a grown child he hasn't spoken to in years. He might say, "Well, because he or she did such and such, I don't care if I don't talk to him for the rest of my life." And I'll say, "Well, do you care how he remembers you? Do you care that he has to go on living the rest of his life feeling rejected and punished every time your name comes up because he has to deal with hostility rather than the memory of you as a loving parent?" And he'll say, "That's not fair after all I did for him." And I'll say, "But that's not what he's going to remember."

So oftentimes the process is one of helping the person who is dying to continue to look forward, even when he's not going to be here. This is his last chance to influence the future. And that becomes a really important reason for someone to work with something he hasn't been able to work with before.

JW: *Tell me about your own near-death experience.*

CPH: It happened when I was a young woman, 24, during childbirth. A commonly used drug, sodium pentothal, was administered to me. All of a sudden, I found myself out of my physical body, looking down. I remember seeing a person on the table and thinking, "Who is that?" That's me! Well if that's me down there, how can I be up here? I was aware of myself floating in the room. I saw my child born, saw it was a little girl. Then there was a sound like a rush of wind, and suddenly I found myself within the rushing sound. Then I moved out of that place and found myself standing in a light. It was the brightest light you can imagine, pulsating. Each time the light pulsated, I felt love, sustaining love. It was like the most liquid kind of love, but it was also like thought. The light was penetrating. It seemed to be intelligence — not words, just thoughts. As I stood in that light, it was as if every thought that formed in my mind was responded to. One of the responses I remember particularly well was: *Death makes no difference. Don't concern yourself, don't be uncomfortable with death. Life is going to go on. Life is bigger than you have ever understood it.*

JW: *Was the light you experienced connected with a figure or personality or was it totally impersonal?*

CPH: It wasn't a figure or personality. It was a field of pure being. But it talked to me, it spoke my mind. And one of the important things it said was, "If you are, you will always be." That has always been so important. To truly realize your present existence is to step out of time into timeless being, which is the state where you will always be — not necessarily as a personality but as a beingness itself.

In that field of light and understanding, thoughts that had never entered my mind — thoughts bigger and more pure than anything that had ever been asked by my mind — were just there. It was as if I was filled up with all of that. And they didn't seem to be just ideas and information. There was a *compassion* to them. It was like with each pulsation, there was upliftment. It was like being nurtured and helped to understand life itself rather than just being educated with ideas. And then I found myself back in my physical body. I said to the people in the delivery room, "I'm different. I'm not who you think I am." I tried to share what had happened.

JW: *Did they listen?*

CPH: Not really. I found out there was a blank wall. This was 1958. People weren't talking about near-death experiences, so when I told a doctor and a nurse, they just patted my hand and were nice. And when I tried to really talk about it, they told me to forget it, I was "hallucinating." But I never forgot it. I knew it was important to remember. It gave me something I hadn't had before. So I just held it in my heart. But I was a wholly new person. Yet I didn't know what to do with my experience. I tried to find ways to share it, but no one listened or understood.

JW: *How did you come to terms with your experience?*

CPH: About two years later, after a lot of struggle trying to decide if I was sane and how in the world was I going to share this experience, I happened to be near a woman who had just got the word that her sister was dying of cancer. She was weeping with deep grief at the news. I was standing on the other side of the room and I felt like my heart was going to burst. As I was feeling such grief for this woman, all of a sudden something changed. I felt a breakthrough in my own heart. I looked at the lady and I felt the love I had felt when I stood in that light during my near-death experience. So I got up, went across the room, and put my arms around the lady. Up to that point I had always been a cautious, quiet person. But I reached out and held her and I thought, "My God, this is what it's about. That light loved me like this and I'm supposed to love other people the same way."

It was really a breakthrough for me because until then I was too shy to do that sort of giving. I had never been able to express it quite like that before. It was as though I now had a purpose, I now had found something I could do with that experience, although at that time I didn't dare tell even the lady. I could not have verbalized it for her or myself.

JW: *But that experience impelled you toward a ministry and over the years you formalized it to the point of being ordained and founding your own church. Had you also drifted away from your Roman Catholic upbringing?*

CPH: No. I was very devoted to churchgoing. It was my basic sense of connection to God. About two weeks after my near-death experience, I went back to church and I thought, "Now I know what all of this is about. But why didn't they just tell me?" Gradually though, the near-death experience affected my churchgoing because I couldn't find the depth I sought. I had opened up to another level of need and that need wasn't being met. A sense of frustration began to develop. I tried to anesthetize my questions, and I went through a period of time thinking I shouldn't ask the questions my mind was forming. I tried to fit back into the old mold. It felt safer because some of the questions and ideas I would suddenly talk about were out of keeping with me and the way I functioned before.

They also made my parents and husband uncomfortable, and there were times when I really tried to conform. I tried to talk to priests and I thought that if I could just get to the right priest, he would talk to me on the level where I needed answers. So I went for a number of years doing that.

JW: *What happened then?*

CPH: I began reading the lives of saints. That was an important step for me, although ironically it brought more frustration. You see, during church services I had moments of ecstasy. I had experiences of seeing the Host lit up. Once a priest held up the Host during mass and I saw it turn into a ball of light. Its radiance filled my whole being and the whole church. When that happened, it reawakened the experience of my being in the light and I knew there was something to Christianity, that the Host was something more. I might not know just how that happened, but it was an alive experience. And from that moment on, I have always been aware that a spiritual transformation takes place at communion. It is spiritual food and a sacred moment. That kept me pursuing this experience of knowingness. Then, as I began to read the lives of the saints and get in touch with higher understanding, I'd see that this or that person really *knew*. Their writings kept me aware that other people before had actually gotten in touch with a spiritual power.

JW: *Did you have any spiritual practice other than prayer?*

CPH: No. At that time I didn't know about meditation. This was in the early 1960's. The first time I saw the word "meditation" was when I started reading about St. Teresa of Avila. So I thought, "I'm going to find out about meditation." I went to see my priest but he didn't know much. He wanted to be helpful so he said, "It's the quiet time when you come to church before the service and you're not saying a formal prayer. You just sit quietly and you let your mind work on the questions that your life is all about." He knew nothing about a technique of meditation.

So then I joined the Society for the Sacred Heart of Jesus. It's a night adoration society. I would get out of bed in the middle of the night, light a candle, and kneel for an hour before a picture of the sacred heart of Jesus. I used that as a spiritual discipline. I had several experiences and in that way I felt spiritual nourishment. Now I think of them as kundalini experiences. I talked to my priest about them and he called them ecstasy experiences. But again something was stirring in me and I would feel that compassionate kind of love. It was a living force. I think at least part of my journey was to discover there is a life force which you can get in touch with, not just be a passive receiver of it, that it dwells within you and from time to time can come up to guide you. Eventually it led me to a person with whom I could talk about my out-of-body experience, and that led me to metaphysical and New Age studies.

JW: *You've lost members of your own family. Will you tell me about that?*

CPH: Just at the time I was finishing this book, my daughter, who was 22, and my granddaughter, who was 2, were killed in an automobile accident. I had previously lost two children at birth. I had ten children altogether, and seven now remain. Each of those experiences was a deep grief experience. Each was quite different. And each challenged me with as much as I could handle at that time.

Three months later the husband of another of my daughters was killed in an automobile accident, and in a short time after that my children's father was killed in a plane crash. So our family — a rather young family — dealt with four deaths in a period of about ten months.

JW: *Tell me about your techniques for dealing with the dying and the bereaved.*

CPH: I try to relate to what's going on in their lives. I see certain physical things they should do, certain emotional things they have to deal with, certain mental and spiritual things. A counselor has to be very flexible about how involved to be. Some days the dying will want you to just do a physical thing and leave. Sometimes they let you help them with their emotional and mental needs. I have to discover where they will let me into their lives. As they let me into their lives in different roles, I have to adapt whatever I have to wherever they'll let me be.

I think this understanding is important for people because it creates one of the biggest problems I see with death-and-dying counselors. The counselor wants to be there on his or her own terms. I don't think that ever works. You have to go in on the dying person's terms, and that's a hard thing to learn.

Support systems are also very important, and I often suggest, "During this period we need to have a team. We need to establish a team which will support you. We have to decide who's going to do your physical things, who's your best friend to call when you really need to talk to somebody. What about your children? How close are they to you? I start making a very practical working unit — whoever's important to the dying person — that's going to support him in every way he needs until he dies. Then I meet with those people. It can be as few as two, but usually it's about six, sometimes eight or nine if it's a big family. Then we sit there, all of us together. I sit next to the dying person and usually hold his hand while we talk. We talk about how they all feel. Some people have to leave the room, but they usually get themselves together and come back. Some people will say, "I don't think we ought to talk about this in front of Mother or Dad." And I'll say, "That's what I'm here for — to talk about this. I was invited to do this."

So I move it from being the unspoken thing on everybody's mind and heart to something they can talk about openly in a non-threatening way. Then the dying person can talk about his fears or desires. Then he can say, "I want you to remember when your grandchild is six years old what I told you when you were six about when I was six," and so forth. Generally they won't say those things to a person who's not part of the support team. Having openness and support is important for anyone who is going to be left in the room with the person while the family goes to church and so forth. The team will be the ones who will really share with the dying person.

JW: *You've been talking about psychological techniques. What about psychic techniques you might bring to the counseling situation or perhaps even teach to the dying to assist them?*

CPH: I use my psychic sensitivity to perceive the bonds between the person dying and the team members. I try to see where there are blocks and where there is a real spiritual bond. I also try to see who the most intuitive ones in the group are. I listen to those people most when they tell me something. I ask if they have had spiritual interests or spiritual experiences. I ask about their belief system. We talk about that because I know those ideas are going to be given to the dying person sooner or later anyway. I ask them how exploratory they are about spiritual things. I usually introduce the idea to the group that we learn all our lives about the world of spirit, that our essence is spiritual, and that I will be working with them to move their point of reference from that of being just a physical person to that of being a *spiritual person with a body.* I suggest that they think in a new way. Probably all their lives, I say, they have thought of themselves as a physical body with a soul or spiritual part. But now, I say, I want you to think of yourself as a spiritual being with a body or physical part. I tell them their lives will change if they think of themselves that way. Here we are, I say, a group of spirits spending a period of time in a physical body, and death is a completion of that experience. Death is simply the spirit coming out of that cocoon called a physical body. Our job is to help the dying person in that process of completion. So it's really important that we include the spiritual in our frame of reference because when that person is out of his physical body, our only connection with him will be made in non-physical ways —in our hearts and in our memories and perhaps psychically, as well. This experience is one of having all of us become more aware of our own spiritual self and of recognizing that death itself is a spiritual experience. It only disguises itself as a physical experience.

JW: *In addition to teaching new perspectives on death, do you teach techniques — meditation, pain control, consciousness transference, recall of past lives, or future-life previews?*

CPH: It depends on the person. Some of the people I work with are very restricted in their ideas so I don't get to do a lot with them. For those I can work with, I have a set of tapes called "Meditation Plus," which are for transferring consciousness from place to place within their body. It consists of guided meditations and experiences, such as a relaxation exercise to use every day. There are ten exercises altogether and each is twenty-five minutes long. They are designed to aid persons to begin being centered, and the centering carries over into other areas of their lives.

Another thing I often do is take them through exercises of bringing light down through their being. I guide them to bring it to the top of their head and then down through the body, pausing at different places to say affirmations and positive healing thoughts, and then back up through their body. Then as they get nearer to the time of death, I talk to them about spiritual teachings which suggest that people leave their body through the solar plexus, through the heart, or through the top of their head. And if I am with them as they're dying, I tell them I want them to begin to go to the light. I say to them, as they move out of the physical body, they have to deal with memories and emotions, but that's not what they really are. Just as they have a body but are not a body, they have memories but are not those memories, they have emotions but are not those emotions. They are light going to light.

I tell dying people I work with that they may be in a situation where family members are crying and caught in grief, but they themselves should not get caught in that. The dying person needs to understand that the time of transition is not the time to comfort people around him, because he is at a really important place in his own existence. I tell the dying I believe they'll be given the opportunity for the richest spiritual experience they've ever had, so they should let that awareness of their family's grief just fall away from them. Whatever's going on around them in the room is for the people in the room to deal with, but their own work is to draw themselves to the light, just to feel love in their heart, and to hold their attention in a meditative way.

JW: *Tell me about your work with children and adolescents. How does it differ from working with adults?*

CPH: The thing that makes death so hard for teenagers when it's a family member or friend who's dying is that teenagers identify with the body level. They don't identify

well yet with the spirit part of themselves. Very few identify even with the mental really. But they identify strongly
with the physical and emotional. So their world is sort of
limited and for them, death is much more frightening than
it is for people who have awakened the philosophical-
spiritual part of themselves.

I've also learned that teenagers often can't handle
cremation well, especially if it's a younger person. They
don't want a mother, father, sister, or brother "burned up."
In one case I worked with, a father had told his family he
wanted cremation. But after he died and they were faced
with the fact, his children just went into wailing and
begged their mother not to have their father cremated. So
I said, "Okay, let's talk about it. Tell me why you feel this
way." We talked for an entire evening until we got to a
place where I could see what they were doing. They were
visualizing their father's body burning and they thought of
this as if he was going to hell. For them cremation was like
sentencing their father to hell. They could not handle that.
It brought up all their fears and all their feelings of having
done wrong. I even heard a young girl say, "If you cremate
my father, I'll kill myself." It helped me to understand how
closely teenagers identify with the body. Counselors need
to be aware of how threatening the idea of cremation is for
teenagers.

JW: *After a family member has died, what should be done
to help young people understand and accept it in a
healthy way?*

CPH: I think it's really important to recognize the value of the old-fashioned wake and family gathering. I feel that coming together and sharing at that time is more important than most people in our society realize. I've found that when people come together and talk about the experiences they shared with the deceased, and the young members of a family hear the older members talk in such a way, it gives a continuity to life and they begin to see a greater relationship to the whole than they had until then. I think one of the things we're losing in our more sophisticated, impersonal society is that continuity. People feel a sense of isolation and loneliness that makes their living harder, and thus makes their dying harder, whatever their age.

JW: *How do you deal with young people who are themselves dying?*

CPH: Death is terribly disappointing to young people because they feel they're getting ready for something in life, and death stands between them and their life goals. For example, they tend to feel that until they finish with formal education, nothing counts; it's all preparation for something beyond it. Somehow, they have to be shown that the present counts. If you're dealing with a child who's dying — a teenager with leukemia, for example — he doesn't have any future out there. You can't talk to him about "when you get well" or "ten years from now" or "when you go to college and become such and such." You have to say, "You count right now. What are we going to do to make this moment count?" I think this is very important for teenagers in general, especially because of their high suicide rate. There's too much focus on what's going to happen later. Some life has to be right now; they have to feel that what they're doing is worth it. And if they can find that, they will stop killing themselves.

JW: *Since you've mentioned the problem of teenage suicide, can you say anything more about it?*

CPH: I think that the state of the world is such that more people are going to choose suicide as a way out, and I feel saddened by that. Many young people feel a strong sense of being a failure or they feel that life isn't worth it. When a death has happened around them, they are particularly vulnerable. We need to help children feel something different at such a time.

What I do is intended to comfort the child at that time. If the child is in a family, we'll talk about how the life of the deceased person was positive for the family, what kind of contribution he or she has made. I sometimes talk to teenagers about what kind of contribution they're going to make to others in life. I'll ask, "What would you want to give other people if you were dying? What would you want to leave behind?" I try to help them see that there are social relationships, that one life affects another life. Teenagers who threaten to commit suicide really don't feel connected to other people or they feel all their connections are bad ones. They feel they make their parents' lives worse, their teachers' lives worse, they can't do anything right. Our society disposes of things pretty easily, and that makes them feel they're highly disposable.

I think that's one of the biggest problems. So when death is going on, it's a chance to help younger people see how they affect others, that it does affect a young person when a man or woman in the street dies. If they can begin to feel that connection, it brings them back to a place where they're not as likely to do something deadly to themselves.

JW: *What do you see ahead for the death-education movement?*

CPH: I feel we can go two ways. We can move in a conservative direction, in which people revert to a reliance on authorities. The death-and-dying counselor can become *the* authority and people have to take their word, just like we took a minister's word at an earlier time. If that happens, I think we'll lose something meaningful. I think that what has made the death-and-dying work meaningful is keeping it flexible and open so it relates to individual human needs. It shouldn't become merely fixed behaviors or memorized answers. In each situation it should be a unique creation that arises from a combination of feelings and ideas and insights of the counselor, the dying person, and the support team. The counselor should not try to fit people into a rigid form. It would limit the good work, the healing work that has begun.

JW: *So your conclusion is that death education counselors themselves need more education, especially in spirituality, metaphysics, and techniques for the expansion of consciousness.*

CPH: Right. And they have to move into the situation on an experiential level. If they do, each situation will always be different. That flexibility is what will make it a meaningful experience for all concerned.

THE
NEW AGE
Handbook On
DEATH
and
DYING

1

The Unknown

"Much of our horror of death comes from the feeling (even though it may never be expressed) that it is the enemy of life. We love life; therefore it is natural to dread death. But death is no more the enemy of life than sleep is the enemy of work and play. Sleep makes it possible for us to work and play the next day. Death makes it possible for us to live on. It has therefore a real contribution to make to life in the large, being the gateway through which we slip from the lower life into the higher, from the briefer into that which is eternal."

The Bridge Is Love: an anthology of hope

Death is a common denominator of life. Each of us faces the experience as one who hopes or one who knows. Those who don't know, suffer. The purpose of my sharing is to ease that suffering. I offer my own very real experience in order to give comfort to you, as you face your own death or the death of a loved one.

The mental and emotional suffering surrounding death is most often the result of fear of the ultimate unknown. In each of our lives, there have been fears we have either acknowledged as realistic or have explored and found to be unjustified. The healthiest response to fear is action, either fleeing the object of fear, or turning to face it and break its hold. Since there is no escape from death for any of us, the wisest course is to learn all that can be known of it, to diminish that which is unknown as much as possible.

What is known of death? In the last decade, researchers have explored many aspects of that process. The emotional stages leading to the acceptance of our own death or the death of a loved one have been examined. Perhaps most startling of all is the finding that hundreds of people resuscitated from a "death" — people who would have died without medical intervention — experienced a very similar sequence of events. What did these near-death experiences have in common? Many who remember these experiences report a sense of comfort, freedom, and relief, which they later try to relay to others.

Raymond Moody, a medical doctor and former college philosophy instructor, has written two books, *Life After Life* and *Reflections on Life After Life,* based on his study of near-death experiences. Dr. Moody wasn't trying to *prove* life after life, but merely sought to collect accounts of near-death for study. He analytically reviews, arranges, and presents material in as scientific a way as possible, allowing readers to draw their own conclusions. These little-known accounts are a contribution to humanity's search for meaning in the face of death.

Spiritual thinkers all tell us with confidence of the continuation of life. Their own experiences of recall, conscious death or near-death experience, or spiritual mysticism have given them a sureness. Most of us need to hear of these shared experiences to encourage us as we tiptoe to the edge of the abyss and look into the face of the unknown.

Why is death unknown? First because its veil is so thick, we can no longer embrace those who enter its portals. Next, we have no framework in which to place stories of visions of returned loved ones and of their comforting touches. If we're educated, intelligent, or disciplined against wishful thinking, what are we to do?

What we are to do is to look at death with new eyes. Cycles of life and death are everywhere about us, teaching us the magic formula. Plant the seed, wait for growth, full-flowering, energy receding, and then death. Trees do it; so do marriages, mortgages, school years, and businesses. We call the shorter cycles by other names, but was it not your death as a child which allowed the adult to emerge?

Look at how long man has been learning to die daily by surrendering himself to sleep, turning off an awareness to the outer life in order to live within. Could this be practice for death itself?

Will you remember with me the greatest loss you have ever felt, even though it may have been the most painful experience of your life? Was it the death of a dream, a hope, or a person? Try to allow yourself to feel the loss now. Do you remember how something inside took hold and you began to change? Whether you wanted it or not, change occurred.

This is the law of the universal life force. Change and grow, or die. The flower blooms its great glory and then the blossom dies. Are we not life's flowers and have we not given our best blooms accordingly?

When death threatens us, or a loved one, a great deal of the trauma we feel comes from falling so completely out of control of our daily lives. We all have a need to feel a degree of control, although certainly, at times that degree changes. For years we've envisioned what we were going to do. We have built plans, hopes, and dreams. We've pictured those we love with us all the way, and cannot imagine being happy or having our needs met without them. Now, with this change of events, we've had all this taken from us and we know of no tool to help us regain control of the situation; no way to stabilize our lives and restore our visions of the future. Of course, one part of us knew that this could happen, but we had not woven the possibility into our life's plans. Now, some mysterious force is present, and as always we have problems with our feelings of helplessness.

Death symbolizes the ultimate loneliness ... the end. A symbol of "without all." Without life, love, knowledge, friends; without body. Ultimate loneliness. If this be so, how can we stand it? Death does not allow us to avoid it. We are helpless. Death has the power and what are we to do?

The simple answer is in seeing that in our daily living we have had only partial control anyway. We must find the philosophical answers, the belief, or the courage to go on one day at a time; to keep on keeping on.

Most people equate death with separation and loneliness, at least subconsciously, and herein lies the trauma. With new ideas, philosophical concepts, and scientific studies, we are finding that death may *not* be separate or lonely. Reading of the beauty in the hundreds of collected stories from persons who have been revived after death sheds light in great abundance on this previously hidden experience. Yes, there is the separation of spirit from body, and it surely is rough, but so can life be rough on this side of the veil, and very often is rough as death approaches. I believe this difficult time helps all of us to let go from both sides. It may be an important key, especially for those of us remaining behind. The new awareness of love, tenderness, guidance and caring that is shown from the spirit side brings comfort to the one departing, as well as the ones left behind.

Our aim is to learn to live and experience without fear of life or death. It is in this ideal state that we can be fully developed, expressing our potential. Fear restricts, holds back, limits our ability to give and receive, and whether it be fear of life or fear of death, it works against our fulfillment of Self.

The root of this fear of death is the lack of knowledge about it. As consciously awake life participants, we know, we live, we think, we anticipate. And it's terrifying to think about not knowing or not planning, or even worse, not hoping.

There are many who tell us that the experiences of inner life are as vast and varied as those of outer life and we can't know about this inner life unless we live there. Just as I don't know about everything that exists in outer life, neither do I know about everything that exists in inner life.

Life and death are flip sides of the same coin. I think of a shoreline. Where does the water end and where does the beach begin? When are we asleep and when are we awake? Are we asleep while dreaming, or living in an inner consciousness?

If we can begin to expand our definitions, we will realize the cycle of life and death within. Medical thought offers us the idea of cells constantly being replaced. Bacteria live and die within us. We are always throwing off dead cells and tissues, but notice that we do not see this as death. It causes us no pain. Sleep, the death of this day, is natural because we live in firm belief of awakening tomorrow. We do not fear sleep; on the contrary, we often welcome it for the rest and restoration it brings.

Think of the satisfied feeling of a busy pleasant day in which much is accomplished: the happy-tired of a job well done. Can we approach our final sleep with the same happy-tired?

A gentleman who chose to die naturally by declining to eat was the object of media attention some years back. His grandson recorded the entire process in poignant photographs. When they were published, screams were heard of cruelty, neglect, and sadism! Were we not to look at this process? Did we wish to deny a man's right to finish living in his own style?

Another elderly man, my precious friend for about ten years, went to bed one night and died in his sleep. All alone in his own home, in his own bed, he made the change from outer life to inner life. Many are concerned about living alone, but this man was not. He had chosen to be alone and one day his living was done. He just finished living. He didn't die of anything; he got through living. He had finished the experience on this side of the coin.

When the natural cycle of pregnancy is completed, we call it birth; when the natural cycle of physical existence is completed, we call it death. Wouldn't it help if we think of dying as another birth, a birth into a spirit life? And in this birth process, shouldn't we expect spirit help? This help is always available, and I shall share my knowledge of it with you in a later chapter.

What is the objective of a study of death and dying and exploration on life after life? I believe facing the facts of life and death fully allows us to deal with our fear, guilt and shame in a direct and meaningful way so we can live more freely now and die more freely when it is time.

2

Can Death Be Birth?

"Always, as the hour of death approaches, angelic beings, more beautiful than you can imagine, join the one-in-process."

Throughout the years of my ministry I have been with a number of persons when they were approaching their final moments of life. Each experience has added a piece to the puzzle for me until I've seen it is time to pass on what I've learned so that others might avoid some of the pain that is often felt at this time. My experiences with life after life do not stand alone. Mystical Christianity supports and reinforces my findings. Lecturing for spiritual study groups and for the human potential movement has made me aware of the large number of persons who have had what I call a "beyond-belief" encounter but don't dare tell anyone. A beyond-belief encounter involves seeing something that others don't.

My earliest memory of such an encounter is as a child trying to explain to my grandmother that I was seeing "smoke" come out of a pet duck I had received at Easter. She assured me that there was no smoke in a duck. Shortly thereafter, when she saw the duck dead, she knew I had indeed seen "something." I knew then as a child that there was more going on around us than most people could see.

I have met death as a friend and so have others I have been with as they were making their transitions. In a perfect way, the pattern seems to be much the same. Always, as the hour of death approaches, angelic beings, more beautiful than you can imagine, join the one-in-process. Because I have observed this pattern for so many years, I look for three radiant, angelic types of beings. Most everyone is aware you can feel death, as we say, in the air. There is a feeling of other-worldliness; you might say the vibrations change. At the time of the end, or near the time of the soul's withdrawal, the being at the head usually moves to the feet and directs the process. If someone is physically present and at the feet, he or she will invariably shift to one side when the being moves into this space. The two beings on either side gently rock the body of the one passing. I believe this gentle rocking action lulls and comforts and also serves the practical purpose of separating spirit and matter. The aura can be seen around a dying person until there is less than six hours before the transition. You'll get some time variation according to the youthful vitality of the physical body or the intensity of the soul within. Then, the energy connecting the physical, emotional and mental faculties is dulled and the light gradually goes out.

A peace flows into the room and into the person who is passing. The soul, when freed, rises and follows the spirit at the foot of the bed as if unaware of anything else. For a time, the relief of being free seems to be of the most importance.

Later in this book we'll review Dr. Kenneth Ring's work in which he examines these last moments of life. My experience has convinced me that these moments give relief to the individual passing and to the survivors. I think everyone participating can feel the unique energy present and respect the importance of this time as an overlapping of dimensions.

My perception helps me compare the deathbed process to the childbirth process, with the angels of death serving as midwives to help the spiritual being make its re-entry into the non-physical world. Just as we see assistance given to a baby, helpless and ill-prepared for its landing here, I have seen the beings of the spirit world come to assist in the departure from the earth.

Religious traditions speak of angels, spirit life, visions of saints and visits from those in spiritual dimension. But what about those who are not quite sure about such "mythical" traditions? Those who espouse any religion have to examine their ideas or faith in a new light when the death experience nears for them or someone they love. The major message of Christianity is eternal life. The celebration of Easter is to underline the message of Jesus' personal resurrection and the promise he demonstrated, so all can believe in life everlasting.

Even prior to the Christian era, the idea of a next stage of life existed. Some sects of Judaism taught that at the coming of the Messiah all would arise, even those in the grave. Within the mystical Kabbalistic teachings it is said there are always souls seeking bodies in which to return.

The Hindu tradition teaches that life manifests on several planes and that the physical world is a place for experiencing. In a non-physical state, one rests. Then, one experiences birth and life again in the physical world for further learning and growth. This cycling is called reincarnation and few Westerners truly understand it, much less realize that three quarters of the world population accept the concept and that the early Christian Church, and the ancient Greeks, Romans, Egyptians, Pythagorians, and Hebrews, respected the idea.

As the West evolved into a materialistic age, less and less respect was held for anything which couldn't be examined in a scientific laboratory, such as the theory of reincarnation. Following the trend of the times, the Christians also dropped their belief in reincarnation.

A beautiful comment was made by the famous churchman Dr. Leslie D. Weatherhead when asked if Christians could believe in reincarnation. He answered, "Can Christians dance? Some can and some can't."

Today, many individuals feel reincarnation is provable; others feel it is not. An excellent work with a scientific approach has been written by Dr. Ian Stevenson, entitled, *Twenty Cases Suggestive of Reincarnation*. Most libraries have this volume if you'd like to explore further.

Accepting reincarnation is logical as well as comforting. More and more are inclined to review scriptures to see if, in fact, there is a basis for the belief in the Bible.

Whether or not one accepts reincarnation, I want us to deal here with the idea of life continuing in *some* form, one with which we are not yet familiar.

In the Bible, Jesus often makes it clear that some dimension other than this world does exist; and he repeatedly states that there is eternal life. Certainly this idea deserves much thought. Jesus' teachings, vital to Christians, seem to parallel the words, "Then the Lord said to Moses: 'You will sleep with your fathers, and will rise ...'" The Bhagavad Gita, the Hindu scripture, teaches: "That which is non-existent can never come into being, and that which is can never cease to be." As a theory, eternal life seems to be everywhere, but is it really believed?

It is not unusual for mystics, philosophers, or spiritual students who have developed strong inner lives to remember previous existences. At a point of stillness, generally in meditation, the contact is made and a flash or segment of another time is revealed.

The increasing public interest in hypnotism has prompted many to undergo hypnotic recall of past life experiences, and often this includes recollection of death experiences. When talking with these individuals, they recall vivid details. Remembering sometimes causes discomfort until the hypnotist suggests they will observe rather than feel the death. Next it is suggested they describe what they see as they watch what happened to their bodies, and some will tell of moving to the spirit world in words very like those of Dr. Moody's subjects who had near-death experiences.

This raises many questions, of course, and jars traditional views we may have. Many of us who have, or read about, past-life remembrances fight hard to put them into our traditional religious experience for as long as we can. I know that I certainly wanted to feel in step with my church and had no desire to separate myself as insights and visions began to occur. In time, we either accept the inner direction as our truth and reality, or reject it and believe we are at best very peculiar. Great help came to me when at last I became acquainted with philosophies which spoke of other lifetimes and the writings of mystics and sages that told of their priceless experiences.

Albert Einstein said, "Scientists will turn their laboratories over to the search for God." I believe we are seeing this occurring now.

Humanity gradually accepts new ideas and throws out the old. Each age of sophistication complicates the matter. The primitive awareness that was spirit-based in the minds of simpler cultures was displaced; we replaced it with the power of logic and material achievement. As we focus our attention more and more on materialism, we are losing awareness of the non-physical. The many mystical stories of saints become accepted as the fantasies of a fervent, adoring heart rather than the experience of an expanded mind. The obvious relief or bountiful joy at the bedside of one who is dying when he says, "Can you see him?" or, "My mother is here" is always welcome. It is rarely understood, but for all who are present, it is very real, and not questioned at the time.

Only later does the mind ask its questions, and many curious minds are asking them in our time: "Does consciousness continue? Is there a next stage of life?" Scientists, doctors, ministers and the general public clamor for an answer and all minds are challenged. Some know and no longer ask. Certainly, we need to explore these questions now, and in the future.

If I am dying (and I am, as we all are), I wish to ask the questions, examine the answers, and find peace.

From the moment of birth, we move through our cycle of life; for some brief, for some lengthy. If we wake up to the Game of Life, we can learn to to play it successfully. We have to move ahead from where we are at any one point in time. To do that, we have to let go of something: the single life to become married; freedom to become a parent; job security to become an entrepreneur. The letting go takes courage! Every step. Letting my children go takes more courage than I can muster at times, and yet, it is destructive to them and to me if I don't.

What is it about being trapped between a rock and a hard place? It's life, with its demanding process of change. Going forward or backward, but lo and behold, we're going!

The ultimate change in physical life is death. As we go toward and through this process, it has many variations and stages.

3

Styles of Dying

*"Don't expect dying individuals to be alike;
no more so than we are alike in any other
expression."*

J ust as the author of a book must keep in mind the
purpose of his or her efforts, a major requisite in any
death and dying counseling is to be aware of the goal. As
I see it, the goal is two-fold. First, I try to meet the
emotional needs of the dying person and the loved ones.
Second, I help each person construct a theoretical framework that gives comfort and support as the death experience occurs.

What goals these are! How can we meet them? My
experience has taught me that most well-meaning friends
and counselors tend to get the cart before the horse.
Generally, they intellectualize the situation and give lots
of theory, rather than taking the simple initial step: Begin
by just caring. Then, with great respect, allow your loved
one to have their steps and stages in their own style and
stand by fully loving and supporting. Appreciate the
uniqueness of their character and help without judgment.
This is unconditional love in its fullest.

What do I mean by style in relation to the dying
process? Let me share examples. A gentleman, who fully

accepted the role of a good family provider, moved to Florida from a northern state. He and his wife had spent the winters in the south for several years. He was dying slowly from progressive advanced cancer, and planned ahead all details: to move his wife, dispose of northern property, get a new, choice model, mobile home, teach her to drive, get paper work done, etc. It was an approximate two-year program, carefully constructed to make sure his wife would be secure. Thus, his style was to do everything that was physically possible, and he did it. Unfortunately, he included little conversation about his wife, their children, their life together. When we got into counseling, he needed help with the expression of love and the repair of his interpersonal relationships.

Another example, a terminally ill woman I visited a number of times, asked me to help her because she and her husband had never had a conversation about her death. She shed tears as she told me, "I love my husband and want to say some things to him and every time I try to get started, he says, 'Now don't talk that way. You're going to get well and next summer we'll travel.'" My task in support of her was to broach the subject of death to the husband and push the ball into action. I had to be the "bad guy" and get it out in the open.

One day at the hospital, when I purposely arrived during his daily visit, he said he'd wait in the lounge until I left, but I insisted he join us. As he made small talk, I said in a soft voice, "You know she is dying." He jumped to his feet exclaiming, "How can you say such a thing? Especially right here in front of Thelma. We're getting the best care. If you can't be cheerful and help her you shouldn't come here!" He had to come to her defense. He thought he was protecting her from pain. I gently continued by saying, "She knows she's dying and she needs to talk about it with you. If you are the one with whom she has shared so much of her life, her companion and best friend, she needs to be able to share her fear now. That's what I'm trying to get started."

At this point it was my responsibility to comfort both of them for a few minutes so she could gather her ideas together and he could adjust to the unthinkable thought of such a sharing. Now I could speak of unfinished business, touching, living one day at a time, until it would become a matter of one hour at a time.

When I left, they were talking in a new way. In a few days he came to see me to have a private chat, and I continued to see her for the next few weeks. They grew close; she had the support she needed, and he began to grieve, letting down his barriers, and they shared intimately the last weeks. I am certain he made better progress in adjusting afterwards because he really had shared the dying experience with his loved one.

Only once have I really gotten into a forceful, dynamic battle with a patient over facing realities. This was with an incredibly strong lady, who was a counselor herself and a student of mine. Her life had been difficult and she had managed to hold herself together through a divorce and other major disappointments. She was bitter and very mental. She embraced metaphysical thinking and believed she could will anything into being. This woman was ill for a time; changed her diet, did meditations, studied much, and seemed to improve. After a series of tests, she told me there was no longer any sign of cancer. A year or so passed; the cancer reappeared and progressed rapidly. With vigor, she began doing meditations developed by Dr. Carl Simonton. She affirmed perfect health and had some very meaningful dream and meditation experiences as she embarked on a mission of willing herself to health.

I know many people who have achieved great things using the techniques my friend engaged in. There are many programs, each working for various people in various ways. I encourage people to try these processes, for I believe we are responsible for our own health. However, in this situation, there was no improvement. She kept her spirits high and at one point she called me long distance and asked that I come.

As I arrived, my friend was sitting upright in bed, emaciated. She couldn't have weighed more than fifty pounds. Normally of small build, at this point she was merely skeletal. I saw her breathing through an oxygen tube, and having lost her hair long ago, the sunlight gave her the appearance of a fragile, young child. She announced she was ready to be healed and wanted me to pray for her. She was sure of her will to live and positive that she could rid her body of the enemy. This beautifully valiant and determined woman was convinced her method should be to use her will against the will of this intruder.

I tried to talk to her about her condition before we prayed, but she wasn't to be sidetracked. Finally I said, "Have you faced the fact that you might not get well?" She exploded in anger. How dare I open the door to doubt! I was her friend. How could I suggest such a thing?

She spit out angry words. I began suggesting that healing has many meanings. It certainly means wholeness, a well-being of all the parts of the person. For example, a physically well body doesn't always constitute perfect health at the mental or emotional levels. We sharply discussed forgiving, loving and letting go of the anger. She acknowledged the anger as the major force that had helped her go through all of this; that she was going to beat this like she'd beaten many other obstacles. I made another suggestion: Healing could mean peace, well-being, and having right action in her life. It could mean it was to come through death; therefore, death could be welcomed. We finally prayed together for love, peace, and the releasing of all that was destructive for both of us. I truly prayed for guidance, and after more conversation, I left.

I walked away knowing that I had kicked down her false game. She was only fighting herself, only using the same tools she had used in her material life to play the game. I was sad I had been so direct, but I had felt so impelled. It had seemed so important that some of that "false upper lip" be done away with. She had needed to forgive. I knew I wouldn't get back for some time; the next day I left for Texas for six days, promising I'd call as soon as I returned.

Later, when I telephoned, a considerate lady answered: My friend had died. It was done. My heart was heavy. I had wanted to be tender with her, and thought that perhaps I should not have met her forcefulness in such a challenging way. I called a mutual acquaintance immediately. She said, "Carol, do you know about our friend?" I answered that I did, and she said, "You helped so much; she cried a lot and later called me and talked. She was different for three days, soft and happy. Then, two hours before she died, she called the ambulance and asked them to come and get her, she wanted to go to the hospital." A great weight fell off my shoulders. If the technique had helped, it had been valid. I needed to know that it was. Never had I met such a demanding, strong-willed person, and I had come on equally strong to help her. I had doubted. Now I understand she was being true to herself and I was being the same, and because she knew I cared for her, she listened. She went to the next stage of life with real peace. I wept tears of thanksgiving.

I hope these examples say, "Don't expect dying individuals to be alike, no more so than we are alike in any other expression." Surely the first step is to avoid laying your belief system on dying persons; express concern, but talk about the topics their other support people can't talk about, and show, through unique ways, that you're not afraid to be real with them at this time. It is also important to avoid thinking that because we are well, we are in charge of the game. As I see it, part of the difficulty support persons have had to deal with is that they are unfamiliar with the dying and death process and they need to become acquainted with the do's and don't's.

No expression of caring is as potent as touching. Do touch. Some things you can say with a touch you can't say with a word. As long as it doesn't produce pain, I believe you should stroke, massage, rub the feet, massage the arms and hands, or just plain hold hands or lay your hands on their bed or body. Many people shy away from touching due to the sexual connotations, although this type of touch is as platonic and innocent as hugging a child. It's time to come back to a rich appreciation of what touch can do.

Understand, however, that theories and ideas about counseling don't help very much until we have nursed our own emotional nature. We need to demonstrate our ability to care, to listen to the outpourings, to support another person in some way. If we and they connect in the love area, if we can create an emotional trust, then our opinions and realities may be helpful. The typical thing that occurs is that professional and prepared people try to explain their perspectives to the dying or the support persons from a detached, intellectual level. My experience has proved to me that no matter how valid these points are, the mind is not what's hurting... the emotional level is in pain; death and parting are great emotional pains. We must acknowledge this to ourselves. I have no qualms about tears coming into my eyes or holding someone and crying together. I'm not suggesting I become unsettled, but I certainly do feel deeply, and I do allow myself to respond. My eyes often fill with tears. My heart is filled with admiration for the courage, love, sacrifice and goodness that I see every day in human lives.

I find it a sacred place into which I am admitted. Being truthful and saying simply, "If I can help, I'd like to," I offer ideas. These ideas are gifts, free to be accepted or rejected. I believe people need to talk through feelings and thoughts, most certainly to talk through fears. Some do not need outsiders; many others do. Some can read an article or a book and get inspiration.

Dying should be as much a part of life as eating, giving birth, having sex or doing business. Dying is living, too. If I have to hide it, something is unnatural. I should be able to find my way in this as in any other endeavor. Those who are sharing my life should share my death as well. Otherwise we both miss an important part of the whole.

4

Stages of Death

"Death isn't God's love or lack of love, it's the pattern of life."

The beautiful work of Dr. Elisabeth Kübler-Ross defines the five stages of death as denial; anger; bargaining; preparatory depression; and acceptance (see graph on following page).

Each of us passes through these stages and according to our personality and experience, the stages last longer or shorter or hold more potency for us. I have a friend going through a period of separation from her husband and she is going through these stages. The "death" we deal with does not have to be the death of the physical body. Whenever life presents us its great drama, we too, go through these stages and adapt to them in ways that suit our unique life styles and characters. In the many years I have worked with dying people, I have seen these five stages consistently repeated, although they do not necessarily occur in a set order or fashion.

DENIAL

Dr. Herman Feifel, M.D. author of *The Meaning of Death,* shows great insight when he says we don't really

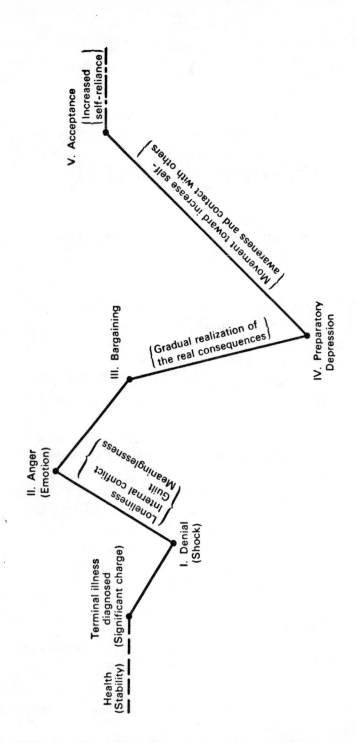

Graph reproduced by permission of Dr. Kübler-Ross.

feel our mortality until we lose our parents. So very true; in our youthfulness, death is usually way out there. Yes, we know we will experience it some day and, intellectually, we accept the idea. When we lose our surviving parent, we stand stripped of a front line; we are next ... and most of us move on, still avoiding the issue. Unconsciously our society denies its mortality by being overly involved with youth: dressing ten or twenty years younger, acting twenty-five at forty, erasing years through cosmetic surgery, needing an affair to show we still have sex appeal. We delegate sickness to the doctors and patient care to the nurses and the hospital. Even if they are close friends, we hesitate to visit those who are terminally ill, not because we don't care, for we truly do, but we don't know how to act, how to cry, or how to face this event. We shun speaking about meeting death. Because our society believes doctors and nurses should know how to do something about this alarming condition, we're angry when they can't. We say quickly, "Get another doctor," or "He doesn't know anything." When a patient dies, the doctor is considered to have failed. We feel he didn't do enough to prevent it. Consequently, doctors have been programmed to withdraw emotional support from the patient, simply prescribing whatever it takes to keep one comfortable.

There are plenty of stories of hard, uncaring nurses, so used to death they bitterly follow hospital rules. Today, many nurses are among the first to recognize there is a need for a new approach. They realize they get burnt out from their emotionally exposed role. These health care personnel are probably closest to the problem of denial.

Many times they act out their own denial in their relationships with patients, or interact very little to avoid getting into a soul-searching conversation which they feel inadequate to lead. I think we can all be helped by realizing the patient leads that conversation. We are doing our best by just listening and caring, encouraging the flow, and gratefully accepting the opportunity to think along with the patient.

The dying patient dealing with denial is exactly like ourselves at other points of denial in our lives. Remember losing a wallet, or your child doing some incredulous something that your head couldn't accept? This denial is the same feeling. Our system keeps spilling out the information that, "These things happen to other people, not to us!"

After a period of gradual restructuring of our day-to-day reality, we find ourselves able to handle the idea of death. Of course, variations of this stage exist; particularly if you have been suspecting the problem before it was confirmed. Many times one goes from test to test or doctor to doctor and this is helpful to the restructuring of our reality. Hard as it is, it's a necessary part of being able to get past denial.

Sometimes one is unwilling to face the imminence of death and chooses not to reveal it to others, pretending for awhile that it isn't so. I've seen great acts of sacrificial love come about this way, for some persons cope better by not acknowledging the truth of their mortality until some internal goal is reached. But the process is working within the person. I think when denial is this strong, the 'stages' of anger and bargaining are burned up in its furnace.

Later, when the acknowledgment finally is made, the patient is moved successfully toward acceptance.

While the dying person is engaged in this denial stage, it may be possible to effect healing by a shift in his consciousness. Such a healing requires openness to the soul level, or openness to the phenomena sought through meditation ... coming into contact with the Divine within. Spiritual healing is the term used, and commonly a person with strong spiritual energy will assist in the healing. The goal is to ignite the lagging, natural, healing power of the patient. If the patient can achieve this change, touch in to the cause and the building anger, and then release it, healing may occur. If the shift occurs past this point, the physical pattern is generally set and deterioration is usually too far along.

ANGER

As I counsel, I am constantly reminded that life energy becomes restricted and renders us less effective when we are filled with fear, hate and anger. These are the major enemies of life. Fear paralyzes, hate kills, and anger consumes. When we are fearful, we say, "frozen with fear" or "frozen stiff." This is exactly what happens. We stand still, can't think, and do not feel. We can't love or care or deal with the day-to-day experiences.

Hate kills our loving nature. Just as the love-warmth within us naturally gives off vibrancy and comfort, hating restricts our precious, vibrant spirit and destroys those about us. The hating flows outward like a poisoned stream, a disturbing negation moving against the life force of others. It kills or cancels out the vitality of life force it encounters. Spiritual students are taught to make their lives a blessing. They are to radiate their goodness, vibrant nature and compassion outward, to serve as a channel of enrichment to be shared.

Anger is the strength trapped and turned inward. It is the fury of the storm suppressed. Anger eats away at our personality until the substructure caves in. The strong body weakens, the fire breaks through in burning words of destruction, or the hostility consumes our relationships. Anger burns like a volcano, out of sight, until one day it erupts and cascades into view. A spectacular event and certain relief, but painful and weakening for those in its path.

A woman I worked with last year admitted her anger at God for taking her husband. Theirs had been a good marriage, twenty-nine years long, and he had been a real companion. Her natural reaction was, "Why him, God? Why not a couple who fights, a couple wanting to be free of each other? Why him, when I need him so?" These are the hard questions asked so frequently. There is no acceptable answer. The reality is that through this experience, both parties took a step forward to begin new stages of development.

This lady, by crying out her anger and thus freeing herself from it, found the way to do for others what she had needed done for herself. She decided to be the kindness she wanted others to be. She knew she had hoped for gentle words and patience, so she spoke gently to others and was patient with them. If *life* wouldn't be fair, at least *she* would be! Working through her anger, she took a giant step forward. The spare love, hidden away with no mate to receive it, became compassion to be given to those who touched her daily life.

Death isn't God's love or lack of love, it's the pattern of life. We will learn that life is just as valuable as we realize or perceive it to be. What is it about time, that one day can seem so long that it is agony and another day can rush by so quickly that we hardly savor its flavor? There is this same relativity about a life. The more we become aware, the more wisely we learn to use each day and each opportunity.

BARGAINING

As anger is released, a person usually reaches the time to face and experience a period which is called bargaining. It seems to me that it is in this stage that many patients reach out for some kind of help. As a minister I get a large number of calls at this point.

As the shock and anger are burning out in a patient, the pains of parting, the recognition of unrealized goals, and the dread of death can become agony. The burning fear of never holding a loved one again makes itself felt and we are not yet ready to face that. Suddenly we feel the poignant pull of those future things we were going to do. We don't know how to face death and we recoil from the thought.

The fear of death registers within our nature; it jolts us to such a degree we now savor the life we had been taking for granted. Day-to-day experiences take on a new poignancy and the bittersweet days begin.

There is now a readiness to bargain. The patient will start to pick up the pieces and either live a spiritual life, find he can endure surgery, stay on a strange diet, try fads or reach eagerly for whatever anyone suggests. "I'll do this, this and this, if in return someone, somehow, can make me well." Many people begin to bargain with God through prayer, particularly intercessory prayer: "I'll do anything, Lord, just don't let this happen to me or mine." They are grasping, searching for something to help them hope. We need to realize that through this agonizing time, many do find hope and answers and some find life extension. It is important to realize that this process of bargaining is most natural and very productive.

Intercessory and memorized prayer become sincere and deeply honest. The response is one of reaching for awareness of something more, greater, stronger, and as the days pass, the empty chaff is burned away. The real richness of life is seen for the treasure it truly brings.

As prayers go out, change comes day-by-day. Interestingly, the change comes most frequently from the purifying experience of prayer itself, not any remarkable or miraculous outer event. The bargaining stage lasts until the approaching death becomes an undeniable reality.

Some persons, well ready for death, have a shorter struggle at this stage. Others bargain longer, seeing death as defeat, failure, or an alternative beyond the realm of possibility. Some, by their philosophical nature, are already living one day at a time and these latter usually pass through this stage with flying colors.

The hardest people hurt while bargaining are those who put too much hope in each cure sought out. It matters little if it is the latest nutrition fad or a spiritual healer. It is similarly hard for those who have no hope. Hope is the elixir of life. Without it there is no light to shine on present beauty. Those without daily hope allow themselves no growth, no joy, no betterment. So, seek to encourage the idea of improvement and the possibility of the goodness of life, if not the extension of that life. The key now is new appreciation of each remaining experience rather than more of whatever life is.

Personally, I do not believe anyone can answer all the questions that are asked in this reaching out phase. I think it is necessary for the struggle to be met. The questions need to be asked. The feeling of questioning must be wrestled with. God must be challenged. I relate to this as the necessary meeting of force with force. Bargaining, questioning, struggling cause change within both the patient and the survivor. God is no longer the one who has sentenced us to a cruel fate but now becomes a Sustaining Presence. Gradually we feel secure knowing there is a potent pattern to our nature just as we feel security in the pattern of morning following night or one season following another.

Obviously, not everyone needs to make his peace with God. Some certainly do, but remember to allow the uniqueness of each person to come forth. Here is a special place and time for remembering that a rose must be a rose and geraniums must be geraniums. The "old crab" will go cranky to the end. Why not? We dilute life to one color if we allow only one style in which to die, just as it would be rather dull to have only one way in which to live.

So let's adopt a code for ourselves. Let's allow the boundaries of experience to be broad enough to include the differences in personality as we all go toward our final moment. Let's think in terms of uniqueness, not good or bad, or right or wrong. Let's try for gentleness, patience and openness. Some days we'll make it; some we won't. We will do the best we're capable of each day!

Remember, "What the caterpillar calls the end of the world, the Master calls a butterfly." (Richard Bach, *Illusions: The Adventures of a Reluctant Messiah*).

PREPARATORY DEPRESSION

This next stage of dying usually becomes apparent after bargaining is gradually left behind. Now, we feel powerless; we are in that place of "What's the use, anyway." Generally what is happening is that we are recognizing it is just a matter of time until death, and often the picture that is painted seems too painful, too disfiguring, too much of an effort to face. Discouraged, tired of struggling, usually uncomfortable, we need some time to make inner adjustments.

Where is our fighting spirit or our positive outlook? Can we maintain our fine image of ourselves? Do we want to, or is it worth the try? For what? Life sure hasn't lived up to our expectations. We're just getting started ... if it had only been a year or so farther down the line. If only ... but it's now.

Dr. Kübler-Ross calls this stage, preparatory depression, the lowest point on the journey. Here it seems one goes inward, breaks contact to a great degree with those who love and care, and spends at least a time in a kind of personal mourning. I believe it's important that we allow this part of the process and do not try to deny the reality of it. I use the word mourning here because I think it's the death of dreams, hopes, future plans, etc. I see this same withdrawal from relationships at the time of divorce. This mourning period is for the death of "little self" and its private treasure of unplanted seeds. It is only after this stage that the more aware human being can come out for the last experiences of the life. Preparatory depression is a great movement forward to increase personal awareness. After this is done, we can re-establish contact with others.

My attempts to counsel families, to encourage openness, to bring death into the center of the circle, are to ease this particular part of the transition process. It is best not to avoid but to guide the experience while the dying one makes his own inner effort. The family and close ones need much help at this stage. Often, we who wish to be supportive make our greatest contribution at this point. Here again, individuals are very special and the pattern differs from one to another.

ACCEPTANCE

One of the recurring marvels of life is the manner in which the death of winter gives way to the reborn life of the spring. From time immemorial, thoughtful men and women have mused upon this wondrous rebirth of nature in the spring season. They can see in it the deep meaning of the restriction and struggle and the rebirth and exaltation of human life.

Let us liken this cycle to the reaction that occurs when we struggle with a dying ego. Tired of bargaining and losing, we prepare for the next step of life or death.

After the struggle, we can move to acceptance, rebirth, a period of increased self-reliance. The body isn't doing so well, but the spirit is getting better. It senses a new adventure and rises to meet the occasion. The courage awakens; now the strength, new-born and beautiful, can flow outward and the family can feel love moving again.

The dying one, at this stage, most often awakens admiration in others. Within the hearts of those who watch, occasionally there is a wish for it to be over and they question, "How much longer can this go on?" At the same time, there is a kind of growing awe at the strength of life, for it has been thought of as fragile and failing. If the loved one is heavily medicated, this stage is often missed. If he is aware and awakened, the insights and perception of what life is all about are awesome.

The brave soldier facing death, ready to go into battle and knowing what is to be faced, is tender but strong. He consciously looks deep into our eyes, knows us for what we are and encourages us to face life with equal courage.

In the preparatory depression stage, the dying one's attention is focused inward to examine and re-evaluate. Now, in the acceptance period, as the attention is again focused outward, he or she can sincerely care about those left behind. There is freer and more open conversation, a willingness to share in the planning. Ironically, it is often at this very point that family and friends give denial signals, direct or implicit, that say, "Don't say that, I can't stand it," or "Stop, I cannot go with you on this part of the journey."

I think it's wrong to reject our dying ones at this stage of their coping with death. Right when the wisdom and character of our friends is at a peak, we signal them to close off. We, in our pain, deny them their chance to speak. We say, "I don't want to hear it —say something else, pretend, protect me, play my game." I want to yell to these people, "Be still. Sit down and shut up!" I would turn to a dying person in this stage and say, "*Wise one,* what do you see? Tell us what life has given you."

If we can have ears to hear, the beloved shares the words we'll be treasuring in a future time. The wisdom and comfort come, the advice, the words may be tough or tender, but here is the bloom of the plant, the evaluation of what that person has gleaned. There is some unfinished business, of course, and the wisdom now comes for it to be completed. The one who needed our comfort a short time ago can now comfort us.

With the patient's renewed strength, courage and willpower to help us, many previously non-shareable experiences can be explored, discussed, forgiven, and released. As the patient has broken through to the hidden reservoir of inner strength, now we are lifted also. The pain is not so great any more. Most of the time the unbearable is bearable and we live more freely. Feelings are understood more readily, symbolic expression is very meaningful and communication is much more satisfying and requires less effort. Rarely is self-pity apparent at this point in dying; most are courageous, especially if death has been discussed and everyone is prepared.

Thus time lived well inspires and sustains the survivors at a future time. To remember the direct and honest eyes of the beloved dying ones when they have worked through it all and have shared with us, even if in bits and pieces, helps us to know life is of great value. For the last "I love you," for the final touches of personality, we stay close by as the fire of their lives smolders, giving its last warmth to us, spreading comfort, love, and togetherness. We send them on their way bountifully surrounded with our love.

If only dying could always be this ideal. More and more, with new tenderness on the part of the helpers, and new methods by professionals, death is becoming understood. At times the acceptance process does not seem to be lived well; it is tough, lingering, and unconscious. Don't be fooled by the physical wrapping, for the acceptance of death is happening out of sight. Support the dying one. Touch more lovingly; increase your expressiveness. Allow this person you care about to find their own style of dying. Here's your chance to love and understand. Our loved ones have their way of being, which isn't going to change. Remember, this stage will be made in the image of their powerful personality! If they habitually look out for others, that will show. If they are used to taking charge, they'll busy themselves telling you what to do in the time ahead. If they tend to be quiet or picky, it'll show, but behind this is their new strength and awareness that what is theirs to do is really *theirs.* Self-reliance allows them to direct you, knowing they do not seek your assistance. They are in charge of their days. Enjoy that part. Rejoice in the strength they have found.

A key for support people is to observe the stages calmly, not to rush or push to make things happen in a specific pattern. Understand the five stages as colors of a rainbow. They will all be there, overlapping and touching, not always visible, not always in the identical pattern, but all contributing to the total effect. It is meaningful to understand that the insights to be gained from this process also may be deeply helpful for the survivors and support persons who must now go through their own five stages in releasing a meaningful tie of friendship and love.

When I lost a premature infant and was critically ill myself, my grief moved quickly through the five stages. My self-survival mechanism kicked in and, although the experience was painful, surviving to return home to my other children became more important. The getting well became the focus point and the loss healed more easily. At a later time, when a second son died at childbirth and I was not critically ill myself, the loss was much greater. My personality centered itself more on the loss than on the surviving process and the agony persisted.

When we lose a loved one, we begin a process of looking back prior to the death. We replay our experiences with the deceased. Using the memory for comfort, we often try to change reality to get relief. I believe this is most natural. However, sometimes we get stuck in the past and cannot shift back and forth. Remembering happy moments from the past is needed to give us positive energy for today to help us realize how good life really is, and also to give us courage to greet the next new stage of personal life; indeed, to inspire us to seek this stage's hidden treasure.

Our ability to adjust is the law of survival. All of us learn that we survive many things we think we can't and many things we didn't even want to. It's amazing how much the human spirit does survive.

Think of the unnatural pain created by concentration camps, kidnapping, rapes; the traumas of being wiped out by fires, getting lost in storms, airplane crashes, wars and injuries ... the list is endless. And many times the victims fare better than their families. The recovery of the victims is focused upon and they often find their way back to reasonable life and functioning, stronger than before. But near them, feeling the pain but not focusing upon themselves are the parents, mates, or other close friends. The survivor has gallant spirit and reveals it. The others often experience bitterness or paranoia, or turn inward.

No one can focus on death and dying and not find life and living more precious. No one facing death consciously, and we are all facing the change, can avoid the realization of how much we yet need or want to do. If you have a year to live, make a list of your goals; afterward, make a list of what you would do if you knew you had only two weeks left. Do these things. We should all be living up-to-date. Have a major goal for achievement. We need to be doing the most important things we can each day of our lives! This way we do not let unfinished business remain unfinished.

5

Expected And Unexpected Death

"How we handle the experience of pain and loss either moves us toward healing or blocks the ability to rebuild and repair."

It has been established that those who are dying must work through various stages in the death process; those who are surviving have equal emotion with which to deal.

Most of us have some very guilty feelings after a death. We remember the person with our heart aching and always wish we had said or done one more thing. This is most certainly true of a sudden death.

We have another conflict with which to deal as we face a loss, and that is our own feelings about what is best for ourselves versus what is best for the dying person. We experience great feelings of guilt if we want dying to hurry and get over with; equally so, if we feel we just can't let someone go. If we hold to the thought that we can't live without them and our loved one lingers miserably, we feel selfish; if we want it over with, we doubt our love for them. Both leave us feeling guilty.

We need time to adjust and release, to work through our conflicting emotions. Even though one part of us is grieved to see the end occur, there is another part which is glad it's over. The period of illness helps us here. If there is a long illness, or old age, we have a time for sorting out, expressing concern, doing some extra thinking. At least we are partially prepared.

The sudden, swift-moving death blow is by far the hardest for most to handle. We aren't ready. We are left up in the air in the midst of life. We have so many nagging after-thoughts, wishes, and desires now never to be spoken. Our minds can recognize that the sudden death experience may certainly keep our loved one from suffering and we may be grateful for that. But we feel the relationship brutally ruptured within us, and rarely can this heal as naturally or as quickly as in the lingering illness process.

Although there is dispute comparing the sudden death versus a long, lasting illness, truly, neither is better than the other. Each has its own particular struggle and its own type of compensation.

When one is dealing with the awful, painful, day-to-day suffering of a loved one, sudden death seems so much easier. But we must remember, with a sudden death, there is no last lingering touch, no planning together, no seeking advice and working out family matters, no visits from family and friends. There is none of the gradual adjustment and release which occur naturally as you watch the body change and the abilities fade with the depletion of the life force.

True, the sudden death seems merciful to the victim, but would he not have desired some time to put things in order? And doesn't every survivor think about this? A planned, last encounter would mean so much. A last kiss, a tender touch, a forgiving conversation could save years of regret and inner turmoil.

When we are dealing with a sudden death, we have more to think through alone. We have to forgive and release. From within ourselves we have to make well that which has occurred without the interaction of the one that has gone. The process depends so much on our own self and usually we are confused and hurt and can't function really well. We seem to go in circles repeating over and over, last words, last actions, the story of the occurrence. We seem to be trying to make it acceptable to our own mind. I think of it as trying to untangle a large knot. The knot is our hopes, our dreams, and our plans for the future that became scrambled with the death event.

I remember as a child, swinging high in the air, a sudden slip, and then the jolting sensation of hitting the ground. Shocked, stunned, with the air knocked out of me, I remember the feeling of trying to reorient myself. This is not unlike the feeling of sudden loss. Your picture of the family, friends, your personal reality, are jolted by the blow and trauma of unexpected death. The blank feeling of non-reality sweeps in and out. The emphasis centers around catching one's breath just as with the fall from the swing. The mind rejects the situation, exclaiming, "This does not compute!" It is now that the basic self-discipline, consideration and concern for others, endurance and freedom of expression that are deeply ingrained in each personality can serve us. Those traits we call character, deep and underlying our personal approach to life, are revealed. The mind kicks in and out; sometimes sharp and alert, supplying all the data we need, sometimes failing us completely. Names won't come; memory fails; our logic refuses to function. As the "computer" spits and stutters, trying to get caught up with the events of the moment, the basic qualities of personality express.

There is no right or wrong way to cope. Society has constructed some guidelines so each of us, individually, will not have to re-think what to do. Too many guidelines block natural expression so we have come now to reject many of them that formerly served the purpose.

Today we are quicker to demand our way! We want to be free to be our unique selves. As a people, we seek honesty rather than the pretense of drama. We are desirous of being free to be. The right or wrong way to deal with any death situation depends upon personal need, character, style, ethnic background.

For everyone, it is important that we deal with the experience in such a way that healing may occur in our lives. Our system innately knows how to heal and adjust. It has done so many times in several different turns of events. Our inner strength can soar; we can heal and hope and live once again. How we handle the experience of pain and loss either moves us toward healing or blocks the ability to rebuild and repair.

When the stunning blow of sudden death strikes, there is often a period of functioning at reduced capacity. Many people have the ability to function well, to plan, to reason, and then suddenly, they can't add two figures or remember what time it is, even though they have just looked at the clock. For these people it is easier to function for the first day or two than it is a week later. When the immediate crisis demands decision, it is absorbing and they can rise to the occasion. Later they find the mind cutting in and out. This is the natural, mental adjustment that has to happen to integrate the occurrence.

We usually adjust our picture of life a little at a time. Our views gradually change direction like a plant bending and growing toward the sun. We move the plant; again it reaches for the sun. Gradual change comes when we approach life one day at a time. Sudden death is like transplanting a plant to new soil in a new setting. The new, different reality throws the system into shock and our grasp of it all must occur gradually.

When one is in a state of shock, the mind doesn't accept impression readily. At this time, so much of ourself functions on rote that facts do not register in the usual way. Forgotten details, misplaced items, getting confused, is the rule, not the exception. It is as if the many abilities contract to a slower rate so that we may survive. Gradually, as the inner adjustments occur, the ability to bounce many balls will return. It is important that we do not condemn ourselves or feel poorly about mishandling things, but rather know them to be a part of the process. It is a natural part of our survival mechanism and, in fact, our future mental and emotional health depends on this process. While trying to absorb events and adjust to change, it is perfectly natural for persons to tell the same happening over and over; or for families to re-run past events, to question, repeat, and struggle with the same points again and again. While to an outsider it may seem unnecessary, important inner adjustments are occurring and those who wish to be supportive and helpful have to understand the great value of this catharsis.

Be aware that we have the same process of blankness with shock as we have in great happiness or pleasant surprise. Remember the stunned look on the face of someone caught unaware at a birthday party or shower. Remember the awesomeness while trying to comprehend the beauty and majesty of the birth of a first child as the parents study the miniature form for hours, amazed at their part in creation. This integration process of all change takes time as new vistas open within one's self. It usually takes years to put experiences into true perspective and to see growth and change. For the survivor, I think the goal is to deal honestly and well with whatever comes.

How can we deal with the guilt of unfinished business? In the case of a sudden death we are miserable until we either anesthetize our feeling self or move through our grieving cycle.

Somewhere we have gotten the idea that being hurt or emotional, or upset at a loss means we're not a good sport or we are weak. Because tradition has strict rules about how to deal with death, we follow the rules, receiving words of condolence, planning a proper funeral and burial, and accepting helpful acts from family and friends. Because we follow tradition, in return we are supposed to receive relief!

It doesn't work. It just plain doesn't happen. So we freeze up and act as if it did. Frightened at the prospect of not being able to cope, we clamp down on ourselves and become numbed, walking, talking zombies. If anyone comes upon us crying or upset, we pretend it's all right, saying, "I'm sorry I broke down," or some other polite remark, pretending we're not coming unglued. "I know I should be over this," or, "I don't know why I'm crying," are repeated to every friend, counselor, and minister. I often want to shout to the world, "It's okay to grieve! Scream! Cry!" We need to thrash it out so the loving being inside can come to life again. We must unlock that knot in the stomach and the tension held in the mind before the love and natural creative thinking can flow once again.

Stifled emotions haunt the carrier. This is not to say that everyone must scream. One will scream, cuss, and shout. Another will sob softly, "Why?" Many get busy, shifting into the activities that must be accomplished. Some need to sit quietly and review the entire life, as if talking through it sorts out the pieces and lets them be filed for safe-keeping. Each of us must have time to finish this business in a way that is natural.

Can these natural emotions be emptied out or guided to the surface in some positive way? If we are to be aided by the releasing of these enemies of life, how can we do it? Aren't we too afraid of it all to empty out? My own feelings in these kind of circumstances have made me aware of the dread of letting go for fear I'll never get hold again.

As a counselor, many times I have led someone on that fine line of emptying out in order to renew life; helping them to let go of the dead bird in the hand to reach for hope and truth in the bush. Is this not death and rebirth again defined?

6

Confronting Pain and Grief

"The only antidote for guilt is action; an action which incorporates the value of our past experience and puts it into use today."

A father of a beautiful young girl, who had died unexpectedly as a result of a short, swift illness, could not get on with his life until she appeared to him in a deep, meaningful dream and kissed him and said, "Daddy, I love you." With this message of love, life began again in a heart grieving and closing. She came to comfort and to heal his pain by her presence. Again and again those beings living in their next stage of life make us aware of them. Do we readily speak of this to our neighbors, or even our families?

How hard it is to say, "My reality is different from another's." How often we keep our secret; stifle our words so we do not give ourselves away. Many numbers of people have said to me privately, "I need to tell you, so-and-so appeared to me and said, 'You'll be all right,' or 'I love you.'"

If death has abruptly ended a meaningful tie, the pain of unfinished business has to be worked through. Several things can help. First, our spiritual belief that life continues may help us talk to that being and release our feelings. Second, especially for an active individual, it helps to do something the loved one would have liked or respected, in their memory. I do not necessarily mean a "name plaque" approach, but some volunteer work, more time with the children, a new creative endeavor, taking care of oneself, or any activity that gets one involved with releasing the guilt. Families usually find that each member wishes he had done something more and they often need to share their feelings in such a way that each helps the others trigger underlying emotions.

I recently spoke to a lady who is employed and away from home each working day. Two years ago her husband died suddenly after a brief time of retirement. One of her major regrets centers on not going home from her job to fix lunch for him. Truly, it would have been a difficult task to accomplish; logically she never knew her lunch hour from day to day, and the distance, traffic and rush ruled it out. Now, she is really hurting and feeling guilty because he made his own lunch.

Essentially, the guilt is a cover-up for much more. Guilt masks our present fears as well as holding us to the past: We didn't realize ... we believe we could have done differently ... we wish we had been kinder, more thoughtful, or even home more often. These thoughts are saying, "I didn't express enough appreciation of life then, and now I am pained about it." They are also saying, "I'm not being as good or as useful now as I can be." If our up-to-date life is full and the actions of today satisfy us, we release guilt. The only antidote for guilt is action; an action which incorporates the value of our past experience and puts it into use today.

Yet, always the close survivor feels some guilt as the result of a loss. The mate that continues to live feels pain acutely and questions, "Why him or her, instead of me?" This guilt effect is even more pronounced in a sudden death situation. The shock of the impact, plus having no time for "unfinished business," magnifies the guilt. When an accident occurs and one or two people lose their lives, the survivors believe they should have done something differently. If an accident takes four or five lives, great guilt is suffered by any survivor. Survivors of car crashes, fires, or acts of God, very often feel guilt. It isn't logical, but it is so. Most of our feelings regarding death are not logical. They are emotional in nature and when attempting to be a support person, we must first do the comforting from that level. After the emotional pain has died down to some degree, we can give some philosophical and intellectual comfort. Rarely is a survivor ready for this in the very first stages of grief.

True enough, the spiritual and philosophical foundation of our lives is our great, built-in strength. But do not expect these strengths to prevent or protect us from the searing pain of loss. They will help us later, in due time. Our established beliefs do sustain us, but the waves of pain are from our emotional level and are not to be denied. It is a dangerous fallacy to think that our faith has failed us as we realize our pain and vulnerability. Harmful remarks are often made by well-meaning friends when they suggest, "I know your Christian ideas will comfort you now," or, "As strong as your faith is, I know you'll be all right." We will doubt our faith if we compare ideology and pain. Faith is structure; pain is pain. Our pain isn't lessened by faith. Our comprehension of the change is helped by our belief system. Be careful in making faith remarks to someone who has suffered a loss. Only if we are very close and of the same ideology should this even be considered. It is much wiser for support persons to realize the tenderness they touch when entering into spiritual or philosophical areas. Touching, loving remarks and sincerity are much more powerful tools to help. When the emotional nature is in great pain, administer the balm there. At another stage, the intellectual level will be ready for questions and answers — the unanswerable "why's," the damnable "if only"s. Then, and only then, will spiritual and philosophical answers help. The rule I try to remember is to respond to the level most in need at the time. When there is something to do physically, do it: touch, help, clean, cook. When the waves of pain are searing our loved one, respond emotionally: comfort, shed tears, express affection. It's the only language really understood. When the mind is in agony, questioning and struggling, use rational ideas and philosophical concepts. Discuss personal beliefs and share how your ideas serve you. Help a person articulate and explore the questions they have. Support them while they build or grow a philosophy or rethink their ideas. Express your continued support on as many levels as you comfortably can, but adjust your focus to the signals the survivor gives. Remember this simple formula: Physical need requires responding physically, emotional need requires responding emotionally, and mental need requires responding mentally. It often takes a bit of time to get the formula working, but it is invaluable as a tool.

A beautiful practical nurse once told me in conversation that she had looked death in the face so many times, it is now an old friend. I have thought about this remark many times and I would note that as we encounter death again and again, we begin to see it as natural and we get over our fear. It is human to fear the unknown. As long as death is kept from being part of life, it will remain the dreadful unknown. As an integration occurs, death is seen as the natural close of a life just as a sunset is the natural conclusion of a day.

My grandfather was paralyzed for several years as I grew up. I played and scrambled about him. He told me stories and visited with me a lot. I do believe he was one of the greatest influences I had in my formative years. The fact that he was restricted to home gave me companionship and someone I could always talk to. I don't remember being particularly sad about his paralysis. My feeling was more, "that's just the way it is." Today I like to remember that after his death, for our last goodbyes, we brought his body home and set the coffin in the living room where his hospital bed had been. I think his life and death have helped me in my work with others.

Death is healing, too, in its natural sequence. Death ends the life experience, lets us out of a body gone weak and helps our soul to go about its business of being. When the body fails to respond to therapies there are reasons.

First, the individual has a block or trauma in his system that isn't able to release, at least at this time, and there is work that needs to be done. Second, the body's answer is no.

The healing force is helpful, but well-being isn't returning. If life is threatened, we must realize that death may be the natural sequence for this situation and individual. Whether we like it or not, death brings healing and release through new life of a different sort. Knowing this profoundly helps us, even though death is not our choice.

A way we might look at the death of a relationship is by comparing it to trimming back a branch of a plant. The branch is cut off abruptly, but around that ending starts new growth. When death comes into a life, much the same happens. An outlet closes and new growth sprouts. Habits change, new interests must spark, friendships awaken and adjust, we put out new sprouts into which life energy may flow.

If we do not start new growth as a plant does, we begin to restrict our own life energy. For a time after re-potting or trimming, a plant hangs in there, neither living nor dying. We know we should see new signs of growth quickly or the plant will not make it. So it is with us: When the shock, the trauma is released, our focus must shift back to constructive life and new growth. We allow our memories, our love, and our experience to give us new compassion and an expanded comprehension of life going on in and about us. I would like to share a technique that has been important to me as I "trim" in my own life each year. I write a lengthy, up-to-date letter to each of my children at New Year's. To me it's my "this-is-where-I-am-with-you" review. I need to bring everything into order so

I have no unsaid, unfinished business. I like the feeling of being current with these loved beings, asking nothing of them except to receive my outpouring. It helps me to let them know that I care.

The whole experience of life, as I see it, is made up of gems and jewels of drama which say, "I care." Touching, reading or writing poetry, giving birth, tenderly feeding and romancing, all are saying, "I care." We are loving creatures. Our natural nature is to care. Loss interrupts the flow. We become blocked; we lose our outlet. We only continue in health and radiance if we find a new opportunity to pour out.

Whenever people love, there is a shine to them. The energy passing freely through shows in vibrant expression. When we become tense and strained, restricted, the glow diminishes. We must embrace and care in order to get healed. To become well in ourselves, we must know we still care and it's okay to do so. But how do we do this? We can whisper a message into the breeze and know it goes somewhere, or we can touch a child with tenderness, but we must sprout the new branches of life that show us healthy and living.

I want to be able to remember the happy times of my past. I don't want to put them away in a trunk, afraid to sort through them. If the grief isn't done, every time we think of the trunk in storage, or see a picture and remember, we deny a part of our life. We stifle our loving self and deny the value of the person or the experience in our life. The major reason to work through our grief is so that we can happily view the beauty each experience has brought to the whole. To be able to recall with joy the love given to us or the experience assimilated, makes us greater and stronger. We are offered the challenge of life's value system. Can we expand to be greater through this experience?

❧   ❧   ❧

SUGGESTIONS FOR SURVIVORS

1. Have an advisor for your financial and legal problems. Don't think you can do it yourself. Few people can truly function at their best for a minimum of six months; it is more often eighteen months or more before one functions at his usual level of performance.

2. Do not change your residence just to create a new environment. There is a lot of basic security in the old pattern even though it is lonely and different. A familiar, daily pattern or life style supports us in our adjustment. Old neighbors and neighborhoods can comfort us and our ineffectiveness is better tolerated here than in new and strange places. Moving in with other family members often starts out with good intentions and high expectations. Rarely does this work out as ideally as it is hoped. It usually is better to do at least a major part of you adjustment before such a move is considered.

3. As a survivor, while you are making internal adjustments, you are also having to deal with the projections of others. In regular daily communication, people are always trying to clarify themselves to others; explaining,

performing, and restating positions, hoping others will know their point of view, their reality. Now, as a survivor, you are faced with the projected fears, frustrations, expectations and old patterns of thinking of all the persons with whom you come in contact. All decisions you discuss openly will have to be seen in the light of others' projections. If you have an advisor, use that person, but know that if you bring up a subject or problem, it is an invitation to the listener to feel that they are being asked to advise you. If you don't want to get another's advice, keep quiet. This will work with some, and at the least, it will slow down the advisors. Whether asked or not, people tend to have a stereotyped picture of the survivor, of how he or she should act, respond, or behave. This is the projection you will have to fight through to find your own rightful pattern.

4. You need to talk and talk. The support persons who can help most need to be patient and ready to hear the sad story again and again. The new reality is being programmed into the understanding. This period may be longer or shorter according to individuals, but be aware that it is a necessary state, and you will require someone who will love you, support you and listen to you.

5. As you experience loss, it is frightening to find such vulnerability within your own nature. Even the strongest of us will have moments of eggshell fragility and we cannot help but be stunned. Our confidence will come and go. At moments, decision-making comes easy and then the mind seems to sputter, forget, or malfunction. A face and name of many years ago comes easily but a

neighbor frequently visited produces no name at all. Events of long ago are easily recalled; yesterday eludes us. This is a natural pattern to cope with and to understand as best you can, while you walk through the days of re-stabilizing. The scattered feelings and ineffective functioning will scare you and tend to create doubt about your capability. Know this behavior pattern is common and do not be overly shaken when it occurs.

7

Living With Change

"As some have dared to walk into the pain of others, wading right through it all, they have found themselves transformed."

There are deaths other than physical of which we need to be aware. A perfect example of another kind of death is divorce. Somehow, because the marital experience didn't work out ideally, the whole experience tends to be labeled as unsatisfactory. How common the expression, "I had a bad marriage." Let me share with you another response: A beautiful, live-wire lady I know answers questions about her divorced marital status with, "Successfully completed." How I wish we could all see past relationships as positively as she does.

As with death, divorce presents us the same opportunity for growth, adjustment and failure. Note the similarities. In divorce, the marriage is the patient. Suppose both parties care, do all they can, perhaps get assistance from a counselor (which is like taking the patient to the doctor to get professional help), and try all the prescriptions, but still the marriage dies. We see the couple experience (1) Denial, (2) Anger, (3) Bargaining, (4)

Depression, (5) Acceptance. This death process works much the same for individuals, for partnerships, for hopes and dreams, and for other kinds of cycles. Life is created to provoke growth and to give us awareness, whether we want it or not! How we react, how healthily we spring back, or how much negativity we can release from us, become the vital issues.

Divorce may literally kill people. With hopes crushed, with no reason to live, many people become less and less giving. The giving of self on an individual basis is charging our current of life force. It adds to our sparkle like a diamond being burnished; the light grows brighter. When we are no longer needed or when we are filled with resentment and bitterness, begrudgingly responding to another's prompting, we restrict our free-flowing, natural life force and we diminish. Our lives lose sparkle and lustre; we are dying. If we could satisfactorily complete relationships and move on, loving, caring, not judging nor condemning one another, nor holding resentment, we could be *wiser* from the experience and file it as a "Lesson learned" from the Divine School of Experience.

The law of life is change. Go forward, or go backward. The vitality of life streams from within us or begins to go out. Light going out is the beginning of death.

The big struggle with this forward movement of life is that we have some problem staying in the Here-and-Now. We tend to drop back into times past and rehash those impossible-to-repeat moments, and often we do this to the point of masochism.

We need to recognize that forgiveness is a part of the challenge of facing life, and thus death. "Why didn't I do so-and-so?" or "If I had only known!" fill the conversation of each one working through guilt, self-punishment, resentment, anger, and loneliness. What we are actually saying is, "I wish I had better savored the experience when I had the chance."

So! Let's get the message! Let's more and more savor the experience of today. This very day is the time we're going to review down the road a bit. Right now, to get the beautiful experience of being here now, alive and alert, lay this book down and go call someone and tell him or her that you care. Share with someone that today your life is better because of the friendship, support, and pleasure the two of you share. Or, write a note expressing your appreciation of someone's impact on you.

The consciousness of living each day totally makes life worth it. Life very full, happily unfolding, makes itself so positive, the pains have compensation. Savoring our food as we eat is a very common idea. Living life day-by-day is the same approach.

There is a loosely-knit movement called the Praise-to-the-Living Club which suggests we each actively recognize the individuals who contribute in so many ways to our lives. The idea is to take the time, now, today, to write a letter to those people who are adding greatly to one's own life or to the lives of others. Lay this book down and think of those individuals you wish to thank. Encouraging people now, on a tough day, is much more meaningful than a spray of flowers on their casket later. Writing someone, expressing appreciation for their service, mannerisms, or inspiration, explaining what they have meant to you, make you a member of this worthy Praise-to-the-Living Club. And think of how wonderful you would feel if you got this kind of a boost while working diligently. What a rich reward!

If we can learn to live up-to-date in this manner, when ends of cycles occur, we won't have such guilt feelings and/or unfinished business with which to deal.

The Be-Here-Now consciousness attempts to retrain us to live one day at a time. "Today is the first day of the rest of your life" implies the same thing. Unless we relate to today as a valuable opportunity to use, rather than a time to get through, hoping that tomorrow will change what is unpleasant about today, we will find whole segments of our lives routinely moved through, unappreciated, and for all practical purposes un-lived.

There is a dreadful saying: "Some people are already dead; they just don't know it." Crude, but oh-so-truthful. The physical body form keeps on, but the spirit, drive, and appreciating consciousness have died from lack of use.

One of the reasons it is so difficult for both professionals and friends or relatives to be good support persons, is that it is hard dealing with the pain that gets stirred up. Let's look at it this way. A friendly, sensitive person sees someone suffering — grieving. The kind one steps up and tries to help, if in no other way than just by listening. And what happens? Too often, as the nice person listens, he starts hurting. Remembering a similar situation in his own past, that old hurt comes back and stinging anew, the pain causes him to pull back and lock off his feelings again. Now he's learned it is better not to try to share or even to listen.

A major change of approach offered by new age ideas suggests that people should work through pain and fears rather than swallow them. A counselor filled with pain will be unable to work properly because of the personal trauma held within. A support person, fearful and distraught, is simply not a support person.

I like the term support person and I use it in its broadest meaning. If I'm your friend and you are suffering, perhaps I can be supportive to you as you cope. I can listen, relieve some responsibilities, do chores, and let you feel my caring. You know I care. You know you have someone to whom you can turn, on whom you can bet. If I'm your friend and if you try to talk to me and I get quiet, withdraw, and even disappear from your life, you are alone. The fact that I could be a friend in a social setting and absent at other times, causes you to feel deserted; you feel guilty for talking about the unpleasant things of life and for letting down the facade that everything is fine. The social code is violated and to get my friendship back mens you had better shape up!

Today, a better understanding of human nature is developing. We are now realizing with a more profound awareness that there is something to be gained by a new openness to grief and to the other traumas of life. As some have dared to walk into the pain of others, wading right through it all, they have found themselves transformed. By allowing the pain of another to be mirrored in their own feeling nature, by allowing past hurt to surface and looking straight into it, their own pain has begun to clear. We find ourselves healed by encouraging another who is tired and worn to know a new day can and will come, and by sharing our understanding that life does get better, that hope dawns again in time. We cannot take the grief away, but in our own caring nature, we burn through our old pain, find loving concern, and bring back our own tenderness. As one truly has this experience, he is re-energized. Such sharing, certainly a part of the basis of Alcoholics Anonymous, Parents Without Partners, Parents of Handicapped Children, the Hospice Movement, and groups of women who have had mastectomies, proves the value of the banding together of those who, having tasted the pain, are determined not to let another go through it alone.

Remember, all parties grow. Each of us has lived with skeletons in our closets until, in the support process, we're no longer afraid of exposing ourselves, and when we willingly open the door, we find most of those skeletons dissipate.

A support person may or may not be a professional. Most of the time this is not a formal title, but is found in the hearts and minds of individuals. In time I hope all people in helping, professional roles will really be support people.

Whether we are grieving persons or support people, we can benefit by recognizing stress in our lives and learning to cope with it. Dr. Thomas H. Holmes took a list of everyday experiences and gave each a point value according to its trauma potency, in order to aid us in recognizing the amount of trauma we are dealing with in our lives. He concluded that stress and trauma contribute considerably to the likelihood of developing a serious illness. Interestingly, almost all of the major trauma indicators involve the ending of a cycle (remember, this is dealing with a death of some kind). The list follows and as you read it, think of the effort expended in ending and beginning cycles.

Death of spouse	100
Divorce	73
Marital separation	65
Jail term	63
Death of close family member	63
Personal injury or illness	53
Marriage	50
Fired from work	47
Marital reconciliation	45
Retirement	45
Change in family member's health	44
Pregnancy	40
Sex difficulties	39
Addition to family	39
Business readjustment	39
Change in financial status	38
Death of close friend	37
Change to different line of work	36
Change in number of marital arguments	35
Foreclosure of mortgage or loan	30
Change in work responsibilities	29
Son or daughter leaving home	29
Trouble with in-laws	29
Outstanding personal achievement	28
Spouse begins or stops working	26
Starting or finishing school	26

Change in living conditions	25
Revision of personal habits	24
Trouble with boss	23
Change in work hours, conditions	20
Change in residence	20
Change in schools	20
Change in recreational habits	19
Change in church activities	19
Change in social activities	19
Change in sleeping habits	16
Change in number of family gatherings	15
Vacation	13
Christmas season	12
Minor violation of the law	11

(Thomas Holmes, Journal of Psychosomatic Research.)

All of these events are natural parts of everyday life experiences and most will affect each of us from time to time. Recognizing their impact, we can learn to guide our lives with some new awareness, for we do have choices about some of these matters; for example, moving our residence or changing jobs. We can be alerted to the fact that we are in an "overload" situation and need to wait before we add to the difficulties. In this way we can help to head off some problems and/or illnesses.

8

Suicide

"Can we love enough to refrain from judging?"

M any life events are set in motion by factors beyond our control. One of the most painful of these for survivors occurs when someone they love has taken his or her own life. These loving individuals are sincerely grieving for those who have made the conscious choice to end their physical life as they were experiencing it, to opt for something else. I believe this matter may be one of life's most anguish-filled experiences for the victim and for those remaining on the physical side.

To start with, my experience makes me believe that just as life offers a variety of experiences, death or transition does also. I have come to believe that after their suicide, the souls find a time of sleep or unconsciousness into which to sink or rest for a time, unless they are terribly disturbed by their own act.

I've heard the term "twilight zone" used for the plane where people who have committed suicide abide while the balance of their physical plane energy is used up or released so they can truly complete their pulling away from our dimension. With great compassion for those in this area, we must realize that they encountered more pain in their lives than they believed they could handle, or they would not have wished for death. I believe it is this discouragement and negative attitude which binds the suicide to the sleeping state in that twilight zone.

One popular belief is that suicides suffer in the next stage of life for a given period of time. According to the fundamentalist, this time period is forever. Some others think the time period lasts until what would have been the natural time of the individual's physical ending. This time period is generally regarded as a kind of purgatory or penance designed by divine law to educate personalities not to violate the gift of life.

Ideas about the nature of this time range from quite ugly pictures of suffering and anguish to the sleeping or resting idea of a dull or somewhat subdued plane of waiting.

I am convinced we can send love and prayers to a suicide victim just as to any other deceased person. I suggest these are even more important because this loved one needs a stream of continued love and positive energy to help dissolve the negativity that surrounds him or her, both before and after death.

It is generally believed this netherworld is the overlapping of physical and spiritual existence, a cusp area. The deceased is no longer a part of the physical, material plane with a physical body through which to channel his spirit and yet is not entirely free of the allotted life force given him at his acceptance of incarnation. This concept implies that the spirit entering a body is obligated to experience and do the best it can under all circumstances encountered. To violate this trust is taught as ignorance of divine law, and thus the lesson of respect must be learned.

The purpose of divine law is always to aid us in finding our higher nature. We might say God's will is to help us recognize the Oneness of all life. Also, through our process of living, we learn to submit our wills to the higher will. The lesson of living through our periods of trial and darkness to reach the awareness of a new realization is the repeated test life brings. Suicide is the willful act of rejecting life's unfolding pattern and taking matters into your own hands. I believe most of those guilty of such acts envision a nice, long, peaceful sleep. I feel most people distraught enough to choose this path are in fact crying out for help, rest, and relief. I also feel most of these people act out of pain.

I believe that after death occurs, these beings sink into some kind of rest until they begin to stir and again seek experience. If they retain consciousness, even in a faulty or inhibited manner, they will in time move again to know life.

There is a story that Beings of Light and Love move through the twilight zone carrying a bell and a light. They ring the bell and watch for response from sleeping entities. Anyone who responds to the bell is awakening and then can be helped. Should these beings make an effort to turn their attention to anything outside of their own pain, they will immediately be assisted by the more aware Ones.

Think of this process in the way we know life here in our physical world. Most of us will try to help another if we recognize the need. Those who have the need must give some signal or request to help us know they would welcome our efforts. Once again, we see a pattern of life which demands that one give in order to receive!

Those who rejected life in its physical fullness have to be ready to reach out and again become part of it all before anyone is allowed to violate their isolation.

I see love and prayers as streams of positive energy we can continue to direct to suicides to help neutralize the painful feelings that drove them to make such a choice. In addition, through the witnessing of the grief they have caused their loved ones, the victims probably incurred additional grief and guilt.

A great effort on our part must be made to forgive the state of ignorance in this area for both the living and for those who have taken their lives. We must consider that the victim acted out of mental, emotional, and/or physical pain and that we weren't able to help much because we didn't realize the intensity of pain or the immediacy of the situation. We, the living, usually are challenged to forgive the suicide for denying us our chance to respond to their need. Also, we have a great need to forgive ourselves for our inadequacy. The great test here is to love unconditionally; to love this precious one regardless of any circumstance.

In all our struggles with relationships, we learn there is a point where we release others to a pattern of their own making. Most of us would choose to protect a loved one from their hard life lessons. We tell them what to do and what not to do. We threaten, influence, and manipulate to the best of our ability, but often, the wilfulness of the individual moves into a pattern of which we do not approve. At this point unconditional love requires release and heartfelt love. The suicide situation truly calls for this letting go and allowing.

Continued grief for years does neither ourself nor our loved one any good. Being a positive, loving person while remembering them in thought and in prayer can be of help. This may be our life challenge now: Can we love enough to refrain from judging either them or ourself as life goes on? Some have suggested that an untimely death is a premature birth into the next world and must have special care as does the premature birth of a baby in our world. I like this idea, and yes, I do believe there is a different experience for those who abort our side of life through their free will. I feel, however, that this is one of life's many lessons through which we all learn and grow. Holding this thought, I feel aware ones love, grow, and trust the divine mind to care for all creation in a just manner. I have learned to "trust the word," knowing it makes allowance for those blanks in my understanding. I believe the discouragement, lack of purpose, and limited vision that can cause suicide have to be met and worked through by these precious souls and that a way opens for them to find the resolute strength for this in time. First, these souls need a period of rest, the permission to turn off to it all, until attention is again drawn outward and they can experience other than personality pain. The attachments from personality are strong and outward. The path inward, soul-ward, is not yet free-flowing or suicide would not have happened. The personality attraction is to look out for assistance, comfort, and even entertainment. Remember the story of the bell, light, or Being that awakens outward interest and thus enables the process of ongoing evaluation to continue. Those more highly evolved spirits, who work as the Beings of Light and Love at this level, bring peace, comfort, and guidance to the one now ready to awaken. They begin the adjustment to a new way of life and the crisis is passed.

Yes, they have erred in lack of judgement, but we all err. This lesson, probably one of life's most difficult for survivors to handle, requires continuing love rather than condemnation. The premature infant requires special handling and this kind of loss also requires special handling and understanding for the survivors.

A good rule to remember is that in spiritual thought, light and awareness are as related as darkness and ignorance. Symbolic language speaks of being cut off from light as painful and of an absence of awareness as being in a place of darkness. Some of this must be taken into consideration in trying to comprehend the meaning of revelation and symbolic scriptures. I believe the divine plan is so all-encompassing that many facets are beyond our comprehension from certain viewpoints. But the understanding we can gain from many experiences leads me to believe no fact is overlooked, and no soul is living out of the sight of the Father-Mother-Creator-Consciousness.

9

Children and Death

"When our elders die, we release our past and when our child dies, we feel deprived of our future."

There is probably nothing harder to handle than the death of a child. Society feels the death of a child is more tragic than that of an adult. This has little to do with logic; most say it's because the child has hardly begun his life while an adult is older and more ready for death. In truth, older doesn't mean more ready, and sooner doesn't really mean the breaking of a promise of three score and ten years in which to live out our purpose.

In some part of ourselves, however, we do have a feeling of having been promised that our children will live to grow up; it is their right. Early death denies that right and causes righteous indignation in parents, along with the emotions of anger and guilt. Who can we trust if we can't trust God, Life, and the Divine Plan; a plan which includes living to be old?

Many of us have to wrestle through the maze of pain at a child's dying and try to forgive God, Life, ourselves, and our child for this turn of events. Life turns traitor: First it stimulates us to think of joy, beauty, growing up, potential, and then, having us amply baited, betrays our trust. As parent to the dying child, we feel all this but usually cannot put it into words.

There is also the terrible feeling of failing the child who dies. The duty of a responsible parent is to provide, protect, and guide children safely through the dependent years until this precious person is strong, capable, independent, and prepared to take life on his or her own terms. We are heavily programmed from our own childhood that this is the role of parent and most of us try to act it out. We feel guilty over minor accidents, let alone a critical illness during which we may perform heroic feats in order to get the best care possible. Also, fairy tales prepare us to believe that right wins over wrong, good over bad, and that Life is good and Death is bad. Therefore, the magic equation: If I do this and it's right, plus this and it's right, in the end right wins! Life wins and Death is defeated!

The shocking truth, we sadly learn, is that too often it doesn't work that way. We perform the right acts, we get the right kind of care, we make the demanding sacrifices, we grow, pray, change. But the equation doesn't work. Death can steal the strength and change the robust beauty of a child into a fragile, translucent form. Sometimes Death wins.

Pain and death are synonymous for those involved, but in very different ways. The pain of the onlooker is in many ways more intense than that of the child who is dying. The latter has adjustments to make, but once fear is overcome and the acceptance of poignant goodbyes becomes reality, the child can begin some speculation as to a future life in other dimensions. New expectations and interest often bring this child into a very fine and peaceful perspective. From this encouraging position, the one leaving becomes the one loving and inspiring others.

The onlookers, caught as they are, feel guilty if they want it over with; feel weak if they cannot control their emotions; feel selfish if they can't bear letting go of the loved one. All of this is magnified if the dying one is *your* child. You discover you don't wish to get it over with and you'd give your life for the child to live another day. You cannot be weak because you've sworn again and again to be there, to hold back the terrors of the world. You can't cry when you see the child's bravery and have praised their spirit.

As the dying one breaks free, the parents stand in the position of trying to stop the rhythm and cycles of life, trying to hold back the movement of the waterfall cascading downward to the earth, or trying to stop the setting sun. And they cannot.

We look into the face of our loved one and see changes in its hues. We still our personal agony for brief periods of time and, if we dare, bring to the surface unknown courage — or we can run from it all and pretend. Few parents pretend, but many deny.

Parents of dying children go through the five previously outlined stages of death and dying. They are partaking in the little one's death, but in some other place in their nature, there is a second death occurring. It is the death of dreams and hopes for this child.

Usually when adults die, a strong part of their potential has been expressed. They have lived and made choices that created their life. The crisis of facing unrealized dreams has been experienced and death, with the maturity of life, has tempered the expectations of all concerned.

With a child, none of this has occurred. We have, then, two simultaneous deaths occurring. One, the real person withdrawing from physical life, and the other, the dreams and potentials that have been energizing our relationship. This second type of death is also experienced by parents of mentally and physically handicapped children. Be aware that both deaths do not necessarily conclude simultaneously. Frequently the death of hopes and dreams occurs first, especially in the midst of preparatory depression. In this sequence, there is more opportunity for members of the family to experience some peace and tranquility toward the end of the child's life. If the physical death occurs before the releasing of hopes, dreams, and desires, the survivors will have more difficulty in facing life without the child. They are left with no energy to activate new beginnings — "for without my dreams I have no life." This response can be helped by the wise guidance of others who will care and tenderly help the survivor move through the stages towards a resolution and acceptance of lost dreams.

Those who would help should understand the great warning signs: refusing to talk about the death, and keeping the child's room exactly the way it was to revere his memory. These are indications that the survivor is stuck in a point of pain and is no longer living in the here and now.

Someone has said that when our elders die, we release our past and when our child dies, we feel deprived of our future. I understand what this means: The more we live vicariously through our children, the more traumatic is our loss. If a person is not expressing his own potential and is counting on the child to act out this role, seeing the child as his own extension, the loss is not just of the child, but also the unexpressed part of self.

There is an organization called The Society of Compassionate Friends, which helps parents who have lost a child come to grips with their loss and find new reasons for living. The group can be of great help and is anxious to start chapters in areas where it is unknown (see Resource Guide -Ed).

Parents of physically and mentally handicapped children, as well as those who lose a child, have a serious battle on their hands to hold the rest of the family unit together during the crisis period. The old adage that we "take it out on those we love" is all too true; we cast our feelings of guilt and anger on our mate or other family members, looking for personal relief. If we are not careful, we may find fault with every move that others make, damaging the vulnerable, precious bonds of love. Often the depth of our personal pain clouds our vision and understanding; thus we cannot reach a perspective which allows the other people their way of coping. As an example, if, from his own pain, a parent pulls back from either the other parent or the suffering child, he is quickly complained about or condemned. Acutely feeling this as a lack of support the parent lashes out causing additional damage.

As people experience this kind of loss, knowing there is no easy way, they need to make the effort to be particularly sensitive to everyone concerned. Everyone involved in the crisis needs to be open in an exploratory way, to ask questions, express confusion, and ask for support. Joining a group provides great solace and each parent may observe how others have survived such ordeals.

All that has been said about denial applies here also, for often one of the parents will deny the trauma and thus has to begin to separate himself from the child as time goes on in order to maintain the denial. Remember, the guilt this builds will have to be faced farther down the line. If we fail to reconcile reality and death, or reality and disability, the great pretense leads us ever farther into a trap.

I had a small son who died, and later, when a second son died a few minutes after birth, I sobbed hysterically. I had four daughters and one son at home and I wanted another son so very much. I felt I could not stand this — it could not be. In my burst of sobs, an older nurse slapped me to reason. She said, "When one chooses to have children, one must know it may go one way, perhaps the other. Grow up!" My tears stopped and I stared at her. I was dazed for the next few days and finally left the hospital without shedding another tear.

In the months that followed, I turned my head when people neared with babies; I withdrew from the world of young mothers and children. I sent gifts to others having baby showers, saying, "It's too soon yet for me to go." I went through all the outer motions of living and being responsible; I demonstrated that I was grown-up.

Later I had another child, a girl. I rejoiced that the child was in good health. All the time I was carrying her, I was afraid to think about the sex of the child. I feared that my selfish wish for a boy had been the cause of death of my son. Perhaps God was teaching me just to appreciate the wholeness of my children and not to be so wilful.

In time my family was completed. The net result included a second son, another daughter, plus the two sons living in the next life. Only after I finished having children and in later studies did I finally find a way to cry again. It came through joy, and the door to tears, so blocked by hurt, rejection, and abrupt command, opened.

The love-feeling I had in my near-death experience returned and ecstasy was mine. I found joy bubbling through my being and from this place, all things were possible. As I shared, so I received; as I reached out, my cup became filled. My tears flowed once again; first, at joyful times. Then, through forgiving the nurse who had been frightened by my hysterical outburst, I gave up my anger and my long held-back tears emptied.

Since that time, I no longer demand of myself that I always act grown-up. I can laugh again like a child, I can sing and I can play, knowing I can choose to respond in my natural way. That means I also can share my pain with you and you may share with me. I can cry now at your pain, wiping both our tears at the same time, and I know you may smile again, even as I. Love heals. When you suffer so much at the turning points in your life, as you grieve, you need some strong support persons to hold the love so you can get well again within its glow.

Pain, in whatever form, has always helped individuals to come to know themselves better, to find their weaknesses and their strengths. Certainly those blows that strike our children strike us severely. The great personal love we feel for our helpless child expands into love for all children. We begin to realize in a new way a universal concern for children which can grow into a love for all humanity after our healing process is complete.

Children who are onlookers at another's death have special requirements and there is a most excellent book entitled *The Child and Death* by Edgar N. Jackson which can help us assist children to develop a healthy attitude toward death. The book is filled with wisdom too good to miss, and complements the new ways of thinking I suggest. Dr. Robert C. Slater, who edited Jackson's book, comments:

> Even as we must involve a child in the process of dying and death, it is equally important that we involve the child in post-death activities, not limited to but certainly beginning with the funeral. There are those who seem to possess some unearned wisdom that categorically denies the child involvement in the funeral. As a practicing funeral director, I have seen children of all ages involved in the funeral, and let me assure you categorically that children who are permitted to participate in the funeral will do so at their own level. They usually will show anxiety and reluctance only when such attitudes are conveyed to them by adults. Children are fascinated by the funeral. To them it is the celebration or in essence a party to which many people whom they love very much come, participate and become involved, and they in essence want to be a part of the party.

Dr. Jackson has described the funeral as a parade, from the point of death to the point of final disposition. Need I tell anyone how much children love parades?

There are those who would deny the child the value that can be obtained in viewing the dead body and participating in the funeral and being involved in the family rites and rituals that surround the funeral and post-death activities. I would ask them to consider what sort of impressions and fantasies the child will create if he is denied such participation. If the child is "sent away to be with a friend," what will be the fantasies of that child as to what is happening in the place and with those whom he loved so much who at a time of obvious crisis have denied that child participation therein? We have again but to ask our psychological and psychiatric associates about the problem of dealing with childhood fantasies, especially when they are negative, over against dealing with the child who has been permitted to be involved in actual experiences.

In the process of death education for the child, as far as I am concerned there is no substitute for involvement. I would run the risk of those limited instances in which damage may be done rather than run the much higher calculated risk in which damage would be done if the child is prohibited from participation.

Perhaps it is summed up best by Jackson in *The Child and Death* when he says, "When dealing with the unknown, children are often bewildered by the fact that their parents do not know all the answers. Parents, in turn, compound this uncertainty by ignoring their children's questions or by giving long, complex explanations that do not satisfy their children's wishes to know and understand. Children are people with needs, emotions and individual personalities." If we agree with this excellent statement by Jackson, then certainly it is logical to comprehend and to recommend the involvement of the child in post-death activities. (Robert Slater, *Death From The Beginning*).

Naturally, children should not be *forced* to attend a funeral if they are adamantly opposed to it. Parents need to be as sensitive as possible in interpreting their children's feelings, depending on the children's ages and their ability to express themselves.

10

Losing A Pet

"Love is worth the price of pain."

Most of us realize children learn a great deal about life through their pets. Caring for a pet subtly teaches very important information about sex and death and provides an opportunity for learning about unconditional acceptance and love. These subjects are hard to explain, chiefly because of our own pains and confusions. We tend to avoid these subjects until something occurs to provoke questions.

As children, many of us had a beloved pet who died. We shed tears, had a funeral, and later got a new pet. It was highly emotional for us with lots of tears but it may have been much easier for us than for our parents. Often it is. The child's concept of life is relatively simple: yes/no, or, it is/it isn't. The child feels the pain, knowing the pet is gone. Within a short time, he wants a pet again as a friend and companion and knows instinctively that the love is worth the price of the pain. As adult sophistication and a sense of caution sets in, we begin to deliberate over these things. The young child needs a pet with which to exchange love just as he needs food to eat, and the child knows this. The adult may choose not to have the pleasure because it is also a responsibility and at times, a burden. These are true differences in perspective.

The child and the pet experience each other as companions, gathering life data together; the child learning responsible action such as having to train the pet. This kind of love isn't restricted to one pet or even one pet at a time. A loving child needs one or more focal points toward which to direct the flow. The pet serves many purposes.

Adults have many of these needs as well, especially the need for feelings of companionship. Many of us want the unrestricted friendship, the happy greeting, the "someone-loves-and-needs-us" feelings that come with the pet attachment. Most of us know people who have a pet who helps its owners "play" mommy, daddy, and baby. I know a number of such arrangements where people spend a great deal of time and attention on their pets and the pets are as children upon which attention can be centered. In this present time it is interesting to note that more and more young people are choosing not to have children. Often without a child, before they realize it, a pet is chosen and the role is built. I am not implying this is good or bad, rather that it is true, and it will become the lot of every owner some day to lose the beloved pet. And for some, the experience of losing pets is similar to the death of a child. Pets are often surrogate children, whether we realize it or not. Some people plan ahead and get a younger pet for themselves as the original pet ages, thereby building a bridge for the future so when the elder pet goes, the younger can easily fill the space.

However, there is often a different reaction. Some say, "I'll never love another pet so much. I can't go through anything like this again. I'm not going to allow myself to get so attached, it's just not worth it."

With these responses, we are acknowledging that every love has a price. The relationship to the pet has high rewards, but it is also an investment of self. I've always felt you have to weigh the energy invested against the reward received. If we have had years of joy, then the pleasure of giving affection, the happiness of romping and moments of tenderness are worth the price of pain.

As a responsible pet owner, each of us is obligated to perform duties similar to that of a responsible parent. We are choosing the role and we find ourselves dealing with many of the same feelings. The more the pet becomes a substitute child, the more similar the pain at the time of loss.

Years ago, I had a small, four-pound, precious Chihuahua named Prissy. She was more my pet than the children's. She waited for me to come home from work in a spot just inside the door each day and did special feats just for me. She amazed us all with her open adoration and I got a lot out of the relationship. She was such a tiny, pretty pet and everyone admired her. She was carefully protected — never outside without a leash and the children loved to take turns walking her in the yard.

Two days before Christmas one year, the postal service delivered a package and in the excitement, no one noticed Prissy rush out the door. A few minutes later, a white-faced postman rang the bell saying he had backed over her in the driveway. Brenda, the oldest daughter at home, took charge. She went in my room, got my house-coat, and wrapped Prissy's dead body in it. Amid her own and the other children's tears, she called me at the office. She carefully told me what happened. I put my head down and cried, and then decided to go home.

I discovered when I arrived that Brenda and the children had dug a hole in the backyard outside my bedroom window, where Prissy would be close, and buried her, wrapped in my robe so she'd feel good. They had all cried, covered the fresh earth with flowers and were making a marker. They talked to me about how they knew it hurt, they told me they didn't want me to see her injured and dead. The oldest child said, "Mother, you couldn't stand it, you loved her too much." They cried; I cried. We all held each other and it really made us very close. I realize now they were responding to innate wisdom and healthy, protecting love. Children, acting out their natural feelings, are usually on target.

Through tears for people, pets, loss and change, we find some relief. This is a way to let off some of the pressure; we all need this.

In a time when more and more of our society is choosing pets as cherished companions, we must realize this is a sign of something. It is at least saying that pets are important in helping people meet a need; the need to reawaken and express their feelings of love.

Grief, however, is grief, and people sincerely feel grief for pets. There is a real loss and a real hole left in the life when a pet has gone. We can heal by focusing our attention on the goodness that has awakened in us through the responsible action, love, and kindness we have given.

Pets do stimulate love in us. Often people who are so hurt that they cannot love a person, will dare to take a pet into their hearts. Emotionally and mentally disturbed children are being helped through pets. Those suspicious, vulnerable persons who avoid others, often can begin to repair their hearts by turning on the love flow through their relationship with an animal.

A key I have found for handling deep grief over this kind of loss is to count the blessings received from the unconditional love given by the animal friend. The natural question can then arise, "Would you rather not have had this experience?" Following this, I suggest that there is a next stage of life and even if animals do not have souls as we do, they do have spirit and energy, so I believe they go on, perhaps in a little understood way. I ask you who grieve thus to whisper a prayer in the wind, bless your pet, and believe goodness is rewarded. You are better for having loved so sincerely and without guard. The life of your pet has made a fine contribution to your life.

11

My Near-Death Experience

"If you are, you always will be."

In 1958, I met what is sometimes called a "Light Being."
It totally confused me and yet gave me a whole, new
sureness about continuity of life. I *know* there is something more. I have experienced part of it.

During the birth of a child I got into difficulty and was
given sodium pentothal, a very harmless drug for most
people. I had an allergic reaction. My lungs collapsed and
my spiritual body separated from the physical and moved
to a place of observation near the ceiling. I looked down
upon my body and did not know for a moment who it was.
Then I realized that it was "me." I watched the hurried
efforts of the doctors and nurses. I saw the baby born. I
knew it was a little girl. I realized that I was the woman
giving birth. Since this was certainly so, what else was
happening? I felt like a balloon bobbing near the ceiling.
I saw a silvery cord, like an umbilical cord, attaching the
"floating me" to the top of the head of the "me" on the
operating table. I couldn't understand what was occurring.

Next, I went through a brief moment of fast motion, or whirling, and I found myself out in what seemed to be vast space. There was coolness and beautiful, comfortable peace and stars.

By my side there was a Being with a magnificent presence. I could not see an exact form, but instead, a radiation of light that lit up everything about me and spoke with a voice that held the deepest tenderness you could ever imagine. The voice said, "Look," and I looked into an area that suddenly had a large, golden frame. As I observed, a falling star started in an upper corner and moved slowly, gently across the framed space. As it got to the lower corner, it went out. The voice said, "My child, do not be disturbed. Death makes no difference in the pattern. If you are, you always will be."

At this moment, as this loving yet powerful Being spoke to me, I understood vast meanings, much beyond my ability to explain. I understood life and death, and instantly, any fear I had, ended. There was a totality, a completeness in the realization that there was absolutely no reason to continue my frantic struggle to exist.

For what seemed to be endless time, I experienced this Presence. The Light Being, pure, powerful, all-expansive, was without a form. Great waves of awareness flowed to me and into my mind.

As I responded to these revelations, I knew them to be so. Of course it didn't matter if one lived or died; it was all so clear. There was a complete trust and greater understanding of what the Being's words meant.

It seemed whole *Truths* revealed themselves to me. Waves of thought and ideas greater and purer than I had ever tried to figure out came to me. Thoughts, clear without effort, revealed themselves in total wholeness, although not in logical sequence. I, being in that magnificent Presence, understood it all. I realized that consciousness is life. We will live in and through much, but this consciousness we know that is behind our personality will continue. I knew, in that moment, that the purpose of life does not depend on me; it has its own purpose. I realized that the flow of it will continue even as I will continue. New serenity entered my being.

As this occurred, an intense feeling rushed through me, as if the light that surrounded the Being was bathing me, penetrating every part of me. As I absorbed the energy, I sensed what I can only describe as bliss. That is such a little word, but the feeling was dynamic, rolling, magnificent, expanding, ecstatic ... *bliss*. It whirled about me and, entering my chest, flowed through me, and I was immersed in love and awareness for a seeming eternity.

Then, from that boundless wave of bliss, I drifted into a darkness which flowed over me. At some point, I felt my body being moved and I began to awaken. How could I share this? I tried to talk. The doctor patted my shoulder and said, "Not now, rest." Later, I tried again and again. My experience, so far beyond any other experience of my life, was labeled hallucination. I longed to understand, to find that feeling of love again. Some part of it remained in my heart, however, and that part continues. It is sometimes expanded and sometimes decreased, but it remains a sign to me of another dimension of Love, Life and Power. I think of the feeling as one of Love, although that word lacks its total import. It is certainly much more than that.

I have found that when I work with touching and become centered exactly on the person with whom I am working, this flow opens and intense energy rushes through with a love feeling that is beyond expression.

I know it is our nature to examine carefully such experiences. After first being told by my medical doctor this was just an hallucination, I thoroughly accepted his answer. However, when a week later a similar thing occurred at home, I began to wonder. Several times I had experiences of standing some place apart watching myself sleeping or nursing the baby. I became concerned about these experiences and by the six-week check-up time, I questioned him again. He told me I was under stress and prescribed a tranquilizer. For a period of three to four months I obediently took a pill from time to time and rather forgot the matter, except for an occasional longing to experience that feeling of total love again.

It would be two full years before I would hear a term called "out-of-body" and come to realize the true significance of these so-called "hallucinations."

This experience changed me. My nature became warmer and more outgoing. I began to embrace the world around me more positively. My prayer life held deeper meaning and after those few, unsuccessful attempts to talk to my doctor and others, I kept my secret to myself.

As a child, I had experiences where I "saw" people who were dead, or weren't "really" present, which left me confused. My encounter with the Light Being allowed me to feel better about myself than I had since childhood. It took some years before a gradual, unfolding awareness led me to know other people, many in fact, who had had similar experiences. Presently there are several books available which document the near-death experiences of hundreds of people, indicating that this is assuredly an authentic event.

Dr. Kenneth Ring, a psychology professor at the University of Connecticut, says his studies with individuals who come back from the verge of death suggest five steps to the transition experience. In his book *Life at Death: A Scientific Study of Near-Death Experience,* Dr. Ring concludes, "We do have some form of consciousness after we die."

These are the five steps which seemed to recur in his in-depth interviews with survivors:

1. "About sixty percent reported a feeling of tremendous happiness. All bodily pain, sensation, is gone. There are no problems, worries, anxieties, just a tremendous feeling of peacefulness and beauty."

2. "About forty percent had this experience of feeling either they have no body or are detached from it. It is a separation stage where you become aware that the physical body is one thing and you are something else altogether. It seems perfectly natural, not weird or scary."

3. "For about twenty percent there is a feeling of peaceful floating or drifting through a dark vastness, a tunnel or void. It's as if you are moving but without your body. You are no longer in this physical world but in some kind of darkness."

4. "More than seventeen percent suddenly became aware of a brilliant golden light that surrounds them like an envelope of warmth. The light seems to give off feelings of comfort and love. "People are drawn to it. There is a reluctance to come back out of the light and into the physical world."

5. "About ten percent have made the switch and are no longer in a transitional passage from this world to what may lie beyond. A person becomes aware of a world of light. Sometimes people will see spirits of deceased loved ones. Sometimes they will see beautiful gardens, landscapes, lakes. They feel this place is like a paradise."

This is such a clear condensation of my own experience and has been substantiated so well, that I think we can be comfortable assuming Step (1) brings peace to our transiting loved one. Step (2) finds the body and spirit separation taking place with comfortable consciousness and a natural feeling. Step (3) is the actual floating through the dimensional barrier which usually seems like a tunnel. I believe this is the feeling of floating in water that is often mentioned. Step (4) could be called the meeting of the Light Being, the Angel, the Love of God or the Life Force. These experiences don't seem to depend on religions or spiritual belief systems. Dr. Ring's study summarizes: "So far, then, the work that has been reported suggests that the near-death experience is independent of both religiousness and religious affiliation." Step (5) involves the closing of the door between the worlds. At the last moment, some people feel a need to return; the others continue into life of a new kind.

Remember Albert Einstein's prediction that we would see the work of the laboratories turned over to the study of God? It's beginning to happen, is it not?

Dr. Ring's research reinforces the perception that Beings greet the one going forward to the new life. His work reveals both the meeting of the Light Being as a common experience for a large percentage of persons, and then later, the meeting of deceased relatives, or other friends from the past. These meetings remind me of the visitation experiences where people catch a glimpse of a recently deceased loved one in the home or another familiar setting. This experience, although common enough, usually gets pushed aside as fantasy.

Remember, we accept poets when they refer to the spirits and their whispered words; we appreciate artists who paint their pictures of spirits, adding wings. I suggest to you that truth always has been offered to us, but we must be *ready* to think about these things before they will have meaning for us.

Be aware, also, that whole religious sects have been based on the possibility of some sort of communication between persons in physical bodies and those in spirit. Modern spiritualism attracts many to pursue these ideas within the context of a denomination of the Christian Church. These spiritualist churches are world-wide with hundreds of thousands of members.

12

Help From Beyond

*Death is not extinguishing
the Light;
It is putting out the lamp
because the dawn has come.*

-Rabindranath Tagore

Today, the illuminating works of Dr. Elisabeth Kübler-Ross and Dr. Raymond Moody help many who have had death-related experiences. These ideas form a frame of reference for them as it does for doctors and counselors who listen to the stories. We may not understand it all, but we do know it is an experience of many, not the eccentrics or attention-grabbers, but individuals making break-throughs in awareness.

My search for the understanding of my own near-death experience led me to study mystical writings with new fervor. The message of life after death, of a heaven world, a dimension of many mansions, had new meaning. Angels and messengers became realities to review. Behind each traditional word stood concepts to examine.

I often wonder how many Christians who profess belief in life after death, or continuity of consciousness as it is called in esoteric teachings, genuinely trust their conviction. This is the true test of facing death. For ourselves or for those we love, we have to face whether we really believe or whether we just hope. Hope wears thin in the face of difficult living. Somehow we need to *know.* To me this is one of the most important messages of our current time.

We see doctors searching through thousands of experiences; psychologists, hypnotists, mystics, meditators, all are asking. If you have the experience yourself, you *know.* That's all, you just *know.*

The value of the mystical experience is in the change it produces in the life and reality of the one having the experience. It cannot be given to another. It can be talked about, but the potency of the experience is such that it can never really be completely shared.

It was years later, after my near-death experience, that I had my first spontaneous recall of another life. I remembered dying. It was like this:

Lying here, tired, waiting. I've thought everything through, most of it more than once. I sleep and wake and wait. I used to get frightened by thoughts of death, but not any more. I know I'm ready.

I realize the room is growing cold. I look at my hands and they are a funny color. I've had time. Yes ... death is cool ... and death is sleeping and waking. ... My mind is somehow detached from day-to-day details. It thinks more clearly about things of the past, more about fantasies than matters of today.

Cold ... then it's pleasantly warm, soft, and peaceful. Silently I find myself moving toward the gossamer Being at the foot of the bed. Glancing back over my shoulder, I see the body lying there. Is it me? Indeed it is, and yet, here I am ... free and moving without effort toward the kind Presence. Now I know I am dead. Surprisingly, it seems so easy. How glad I am it's done. I feel such relief ... effortless, floating, at peace, surrendering into whatever it is that I am.

Always I have struggled to be free; didn't even know what I was struggling for or against. Always active, meeting the next goal, completing my day's work. Dressing, eating, working, thinking ... now it's done. My book is finished. God, close the cover!

But what is this? I thought it was all over. Now there seems to be more. Where am I? So at peace. Hurrah! It is being done to me, for me. I do not have to try. I relax; I am floating free.

The One who guides me motions and I understand. I think and it is done. No effort, I make absolutely no effort. Pictures flash about me, tears roll down my cheeks. I feel such relief, such comfort. Some memories of the past come and I *know*. Understanding floods my mind. So many thoughts try to crowd into my head, I can't sort them out. I am tired. All of that is far away, so long ago.

I want this peace. I need this rest. I resist thinking back and I want to move on in this effortless, flowing peacefulness. Is this the river that is spoken of? It is a flowing river of life taking me forward, away from the whirling effort— life seems to be the struggle of a piece of driftwood always resisting being drawn into the suction of the whirlpool.

Whirlpool is death and to be avoided at all costs! It ends everything. Then it's all over. I can't go there. I must struggle away from the center or be swallowed up in the nothingness. Run ... cry ... scream ... just don't die!

Now it's done. I move easily, following the Light Form ahead through all the figures, colors, and tones. I have no interest to question or to see. I know that if I want to, I can. The guide is gentle and strong, helpful if I should have need. I am at peace and following freely, relieved of my struggle.

That recollection answered another question for me, the question of reincarnation. Since then, I have recalled several past lives. Each time there is a complete awareness that this is myself in another form. Each time, in retrospect, there are some facets in common with some question or experience by which I am currently challenged.

Several students of mine, making their transitions, have appeared soon after death to let me know of their passing. In psychic or spiritualist circles, it is expected that the beloved will look in on the funeral or memorial service. I have seen discarnate beings at these times trying to comfort family members sobbing in grief.

It is not enough when transition comes just to let go of the loved one. In the past, the Egyptian culture taught prayer for forty-nine days after physical death while the soul moved through a place of review and contemplation. While the Christian tradition does not specify the number of days, it has always taught prayers for the dead and the dying. Likewise, the Judaic tradition has specific customs to help people at this time. The Rosicrucian tradition suggests there should be a constant vigil, someone praying for thirty-six hours. During these thirty-six hours, the spirit reviews the life experience and is touched by the emotional energy that comes from the earth plane. The spirit's emotional energy is tied yet to the physical family, the loved ones here on the earth plane, and many times beings look back and are aware of the grief of their loved ones. Thus we can understand how we might have visions of recently deceased beings, or see a beloved who has been killed elsewhere ... sometimes before we physically know of the death. I have seen several magazine articles about how frequently people have visions of deceased individuals in the two weeks after death. I sincerely believe this is to comfort and help those left behind. Dr. Henry Schmales, Jr., writes, "During the first two weeks after the death and sometimes longer, it is most common for the grieving survivors to have fleeting images of the deceased, while awake or on awakening as well as in dreams." It is also Dr. Schmales' opinion that doctors should tell families about these experiences. "Without this reassurance, the experience can be so frightening to those having it they may think that they are losing their minds." (*Emergency Medicine Magazine,* March, 1971.)

I will include here an incredible personal story which confirms that those who pass over continue loving us and try to make us aware of it. When I was fourteen years old, I traveled from Florida to California to visit my father and stepmother and their family. It was to be the last time I was to see him alive, although for years afterward we wrote and shared plans for the day we would get together again. In 1973, after I was a minister and very much involved in spiritual teachings, I was awakened early one morning by a telephone call. I got up and spoke on the telephone with a man who told me that my father had been accidentally killed. My father owned a business that involved heavy equipment and the caller told me that my father had been on a forklift that had hit an ammonia pipeline. In the explosion, he had burned to death. I was overwhelmed; shocked. I hung up the phone and cried. Later, when I was somewhat calmed, I realized that I had not asked the usual questions: "When should I come to California?" and "How is my stepmother, Marie?" At this point I went to the telephone and made a long distance call to Marie. As I began to talk to her, I had a funny feeling she wasn't upset. I asked her about the services and she replied, "What services?" I told her then about the phone call that I had received and she said, "Carol, nothing has happened to your dad. He is right here." As I spoke with my father I thought, "That phone call was the cruelest joke I have ever heard in my life!" In November of 1975, two and a half years later, another telephone call came. This time a man called my mother, who came to me and told me my father had been killed exactly as had been described in my previous phone call. I called Marie and she asked, "How do you explain this? It happened just as it was told to you." For the first time, I realized that I had received a prophetic, psychic "phone call," not a cruel practical joke. Why? I have decided now it was to give me a chance to go visit; a last appeal, and I did not go. Now that my father really was dead, I had to make the decision about attending the funeral in California. I said to Marie, "I did not come when I could have. I do not want to come now." After I spoke to her, I changed my mind, thinking I would go. But it was impractical, etc., and so I vacillated. Then I had one of the most meaningful experiences of my life as I drove from St. Petersburg to Sarasota one afternoon. On this route there is a very high bridge called the Skyway Bridge. It is spectacular and beautiful, and as I was driving, moving toward the highest point, a presence filled my automobile. I dared not look, but I felt my father, exactly as I had felt him so many years before when we had been together. "Dad?" I ventured. He answered, "It is all right, Carol, I have come to you." And I said, "I'm sorry I didn't come." He answered, "Understand... it is all right. Everything is all right. I understand; I know." I said, "Can I look at you?" and he replied, "Of course." It had been thirty years since I had last seen my dad and turning my head toward him, I could perceive a mist-like presence. He was heavier than when I last saw him, with less hair, but I recognized him and felt hot tears of relief and love flowing down my cheeks. I said, "Dad, I love you," and he reassured me, "Don't worry, Carol. I came to you."

We may live in two different worlds, but I believe those worlds overlap at times, especially at birth and death, times of prayer and intense love. Souls moving forward want to and do touch us in some way to affirm that love continues in their consciousness also.

God works in mysterious ways His wonders to perform and in God's house there are many mansions. I know there is an eternal life, a life-after-life process, and I am at peace with that knowledge.

As persons who have this consciousness of life-after-life continuity, what can we do to help the one in transition? If we are a friend and aware, yet not as emotional as the immediate family, we can love dearly and impersonally at this time. We need to work from an impersonal, spiritual standpoint in this situation. We will send a radiant, positive energy to the one passing to help neutralize the grief of the family. This is to keep the heaviness of the grief from flowing toward the deceased one.

When we are working with persons making their transition, we should enter into quiet times of meditation, visualization, or prayer, sending a positive stream of love energy to them. If we believe that when we love and care, positive energy is being sent to another, we certainly want to do this to be helpful at this stage of experience.

Prayer is very helpful, in whatever form feels right for you. Send love, light, and comfort to surround the one you are remembering before, during, and after death. I usually recommend continuing this practice for at least thirty days after the death.

This stream of positive love energy surrounds our friend and assists them to respond to those helping from the other levels or planes of existence. When beings move from plane to plane, there is a state of adjustment to be made. The beings, having recently had all their attention focused on the physical life, must now let go and refocus on another plane. For this reason we pray, care, and maintain a stream of non-physical, positive energy around them. This is helpful as the adjustment is made, providing familiar vibrations for them to sustain their efforts.

As I have mentioned, Eastern and Western traditions have all contributed ideas for helping those facing transition, for making the crossing, and for holding the love strong between these planes for a time. A deeper understanding of these traditions provides great comfort for both those crossing and those remaining on the physical side. A new understanding that there is a long tradition of deceased loved ones making themselves visible to their survivors will sustain many as they make an adjustment to their loss.

13

Survivors Face Change

"The survivor can no more avoid being touched by the ending of a cycle than can the one dying."

Death, because we see it as so final, intimidates us all. A death touches many people although not all on a conscious level. Be aware that a person's death affects his neighbor, the banker, the postman, as well as family, friends, and other support people. Because people feel so powerless in a terminal situation, they tend to avoid the individual involved. It becomes too much effort to make small talk or to find a way to show concern and at the same time skirt the emotional issues. When one partner of a couple is dying, the life style of the other one also begins to change. One-by-one, friends stop dropping in. Eventually, social invitations stop coming because people think the healthy mate wouldn't want to attend alone. Of course, some life style change is expected, but not the break in social ties. The changes, including chores to do, trips to town, taking care of tasks formerly handled by the spouse, even sleeping, eating, and visiting, become difficult to manage alone. Super courage is summoned to do it all. This super courage will be needed for the protection of the dying mate now, and later for the re-balancing of self. When the time comes, the survivor will use this super courage to make the necessary adjustments.

Both need the feeling of having done everything possible, of knowing that family affairs are in right order, and they each need an abundant expression of affection. Both require hope and trust and awareness of the great inventiveness of the Universe.

When a loving tie to a mate is ended, we feel as if a plug has been pulled from our life. We have eaten together, slept together, and made decisions with each other's well-being in mind. In fact, the lives were so closely entwined that when one leaves, each life as it has been known, is over. It is equally important to realize that a survivor moves to a new stage of life at this point even as the one making the transition moves to spirit life. A next stage awaits both.

When the death or loss is sudden, shock has the great welcoming value of anesthetizing us to some degree. I call it going on automatic pilot for a time. We do what we have to do. We perform the responsible action and then, when all is done, we begin to feel the pins and needles of our feeling nature coming back to circulation. The pain continues to grow until our logic begins to fail us. We become frightened by our pain, by our periods of not being able to cope, by illogical and emotional actions. Our natural response is to hide.

Hiding our grief, trauma, and fright simply causes the problem to grow out of sight. And grow it does. Eventually it is revealed and we'll burst into tears in public, lash out at some undeserving individual, get drunk and embarrass ourselves, or behave in an obnoxious way causing guilt and regret. As we begin to suspect we're cracking-up or falling apart, we may decide to see someone about it and begin the tranquilizer game or hunt for a love affair or postpone it by burying ourselves in more work.

For many people these have been avenues of escape for centuries. They are modes of running away and any and all can lead to greater trauma. I see these as ways to postpone or deny our pain as survivors. Let me say to you that the survivor can no more avoid being touched by the ending of a cycle than can the one dying. If we are in a relationship as friend, parent, or mate, it's two-sided and when change comes, both have to take a deep breath and re-balance. For a brief time other people may share the load, not carrying it nor taking over, but just being there. A crutch isn't wanted forever, but in the crisis, it's needed. A person who has been over the route, knowing how bad it is, can be especially supportive. It's like the young woman who, facing her first delivery, needs to talk to someone who has been through childbirth. This kind of sharing encourages new life to flow and creates the understanding that it can be done.

There is a feeling of a deep hole burned through oneself where the love was, after the loss. This terrible emptiness is, I believe, the worst part of it all. It lives there inside your body in the feeling nature, a constant reminder you are not whole. I have heard this discussed many times. It is like the hole left in the ground after pulling out a tree that has grown in place for several years. The ground is torn and empty afterwards, and so are we after our loss. It takes time and new life to fill in this hole.

It's not a matter of replacing; it's a matter of *new* life. Our experience makes each of us a new person, different even to ourselves. So we have to sift through our life, interests, habits, ideas, and philosophy and re-define all of them. We have to make room for this experience of change and allow it to make a contribution to the new picture of life we must now carry. Time helps some, but help comes not from the passing of days but from the new life this time can bring if we let it. I know some bitter, frightened, and angry persons who, refusing life, have not healed although years have passed.

Recently, a beautiful lady with whom I shared my book said, "Tell them to give themselves permission to walk away from the grief at times and come back to it again later." Widowed almost two years ago, she's healing now. She has fought through most of her pain, has days whole and well and then another time of agony appears. She has learned to take life one day at a time and to look her pain in the eye, knowing it isn't just an enemy, but the transmuting energy of life.

Love and pain change us. They help us to reach the most poignant heights of expression. If I know pain, how gentle I'll be as I touch your bruise, for I have suffered so also. Searing pain strengthens the Spirit and tenderness is born. Young love is praised for its sweetness, old wine for its seasoned flavor.

Part of freeing ourselves from loneliness comes from realizing that we are alone in life anyway. We can only share bits and pieces of our life regardless of our love. It is wisdom to see that most of life takes place inside our own head. Our subjective values and perspectives give life its coloring and we all know that two people can witness the same sight, hear the same words, and make two different experiences out of it.

In resisting loneliness, we attach ourselves to the idea of having someone, a particular someone, sharing life with us *always*. We seldom face the fact that while our love is very real and meaningful, each of us spends many hours away from the other, doing something and involved with the life we lead within our own head. We gather experience for our own life alone. Togetherness has more to do with attitude, perspective, and imagination than with constant companionship.

Each of us is born alone into this life. We walk for a period of time in touch with many: first parents, then friends, perhaps a mate and children, then more friends. On occasion, we share deeply and meaningfully with different people. But there really isn't anyone in our life who is with us all the time except our own self. This is important to realize because our true security is best vested in the realization that this self is the only companion who is always present.

We may choose to spend part of our time and life with another. Whether it be long or short, we become companions. But it's temporary, regardless of the time period, because we are each on our own track, even if our lives are parallel for a long distance. Realizing this, we can make the time shared with our precious ones even better and we can also accept the responsibility for the need to create some other situation when this time is over.

Part of discovering our true way is to realize we can't make others be "where we are" in understanding, outlook, or experience. As we accept this fact, we begin to enjoy the bonus of having our time together, sharing, loving, and appreciating the goodness of the hour and day, not spoiling it by dread if we see things differently or if we go our separate ways. Thus, we can store up the goodness of life through memories and attitude, using these as building blocks for the future.

The inner self is our one permanent companion and to develop rapport with it is authentic security. If each of us is feeling good about the self, and confident, it helps in the present and may help in the future of this life and, challenging thought, help in future lives!

14

Believing Versus Knowing

"Belief is needed when you don't know."
— *Mortimer Adler*

T he dying experience I shared with you in chapter eleven was a personal, beautiful past-life remembrance. In it, I was an elderly lady making my transition all alone. I had lived a solitary existence for some years and was unafraid. In fact, I did not want to be disturbed or bothered. Wanting to be with my thoughts in peace, I intuitively knew the presence or reactions of others around me would be disturbing. When I had this recall, I had new feelings about the anxiety felt for elderly loved ones living by themselves. Think about it now ... wouldn't very private persons and/or those who have chosen to live alone have a different viewpoint from those who regularly need others with them? Our logic tells us that the desired death experience could vary greatly according to the disposition and personality of each individual. In this type of situation, I think the survivor's real problem is that he doesn't want to think he wasn't there when his loved one needed him.

In trying to share with you my personal near-death experience during childbirth in this lifetime, I return to a familiar, old feeling of inadequacy. At the time, in the presence of the dynamic, loving Being, my realization was such that I experienced a clear perception of many things, particularly that life *does* make sense. It *does* have purpose and pattern and I can rest in that truth.

I have spent more than twenty years now trying to find words and ways to share that profound message. As of yet, I feel I am only scattering crumbs of it as best I can. I approach the task by attempting to practice what I preach, touching one life at a time, one day at a time.

The vastness of my experience and its revelations astonish me even yet. I have read similar statements from Dr. John Lilly in his book, *The Center of the Cyclone,* about drug experiences. Repeatedly in poetry, scripture, and in literature of revelatory nature, there is the reference to truth beyond expression. My attempt to express it here is simply that, an attempt.

The question of belief and knowing came up recently on a television interview with Mortimer Adler, one of the leading authorities on the teachings of Thomas Aquinas, the great father of Christianity. Adler expresses the difference between belief and knowing by saying that belief is needed when you don't *know.* You take the logical and rational process to a certain position and then leap by faith to a surmise. Example: belief in after-life, eternal life, immortality. You can use all your facts, scriptures, and teachings to help in the structure to get to that belief. However, when you *know,* you no longer believe. You do not have to leap by faith. No leap is required because you have experience, reality; a fact. You now *know.*

I have come to the decision, out of love and concern for those traveling ahead of me toward their transition, that I must share my understanding of the next stage of life. If we could call on the many who have had experiences that help them *know,* rather than believe, and ask them to share their perception of reality and how they arrived at it, we could have a great leap forward in awareness.

Many come to see me to share personal experiences of a revelatory, or "supernatural" nature. Needing to talk about the occurrence, they tell me, "I've never shared this with anyone, or anyone outside my family." If we weren't so quick to condemn that which we do not understand, these people could be encouraged to share their experiences, which would be helpful to those preparing for death.

Mortimer Adler, who also studies the Greek philosopher Aristotle, shows how, in the refined thinking process, individuals come to a comprehension of continuity of consciousness and a realization of the "prime mover" of life. Adler is Jewish; his family is Episcopalian; he has been responsible for many accepting the intellectual side of Catholicism; and he readily states he believes in God. Asked why, since he understood Christianity and its teachings so well, he never joined its communion, he replied he had not yet found the "resolute will to walk in the path of Jesus Christ." I think this is an example of enlightened thought bringing an awareness so broad and encompassing that one leaps over the divisions and lines of religions to the realization of the whole: God. Aristotle found his Truth through philosophy. Adler, pondering those Greek ideas while also exposed to the finest of Catholic thought, leapt to the realization of the oneness of life. All minds fed and stimulated through philosophy, beauty, and refined logic become open to the power, rhythm, and flow of life. Open-ended lives begin to make sense if we free ourselves from time and space limitations. This means the mind can go beyond the body even now.

The next step, when we dare, is to think a new way, listen to new thoughts, stretch to a new dimension, and if we can get a process of openness started, we can free ourselves from biases, programming, and the limits we have allowed to restrict us. Interesting that a belief in a "prime mover" can help us appreciate Greek, Jewish and Catholic thought. Could it mean the oneness of life can truly be realized?

In any period of search and change, we must go through some degree of experimentation to find techniques and concepts that work and are acceptable for helping deal with the business of life and the challenges it offers. Today, many are exploring new ideas and ancient ideas for their contribution to the quality of modern life. While discrimination must be used in this as in all matters, we miss much of life that is exciting and wonderful when we are unwilling to take time to explore and evaluate. Blind and automatic acceptance of others' ideas is ignorance. We all are trained and taught many things, especially as children, that need to be re-examined as we mature into thinking adults. We may choose to continue just as we were. That's fine, we have made the choice. If we never look, however, we may wear old and useless ideas, habits, and concepts to clothe a new and great life. Some of us are still in that rut with our understanding of change and growth. At some point we all need to think a new way about things just to see the view from there!

In a business management seminar I attended once, it was suggested that we sit on a high stool instead of regular office chairs for one day to see how different our work area seemed to us. Being creatures of habit, we regularly put up with inefficiency and unnecessary inconvenience once we are used to something, failing to notice how it hinders us. To give new ideas opportunity to grow, we must listen, evaluate, and play with them, asking, "What if ...?" I see this as a mental, stretching exercise. Gradually, as we come to find that the hints and experiences of other people substantiate some of these new and different ideas, we become more comfortable in exploring concepts anew.

Torkom Saraydarian, a new age philosopher and teacher, offers suggestions and techniques for living up-to-date in his book *The Science of Becoming Oneself.* I have adopted many of these and use them with students and clients. The following is particularly appropriate as a preparation for the transition period:

> In a quiet meditative mood, as detached as possible, begin to visualize the death we await. As we create our death, let's make it as pleasant and comfortable as possible with all the people present that we desire. Put in

other aspects as they suit you, for as we write the script, we can do it our own way. For example, if you are terminally ill, you have some facts to work with; it you are not, you don't. So begin to create the ending of this stage of life and prepare for the beginning of the new.

Now visualize yourself in the coffin, family members reacting to the news of your death, friends helpful and tearful. Be conscious of business matters that would fall upon others, perhaps property and possessions that would have to be disposed of. What else does your particular life ending leave "up in the air"? As you get strong resistance to these thoughts, know this is perfectly natural. Most of us resist doing such thinking because it is unpleasant and it is a lot of work. In this relaxed and detached awareness, be open to thoughts of your inner nature. Do you need to give some kind word to another? Do you need to forgive another or release another from a debt? Who really cares for you that you fail to recognize? Would you like to leave something to a particular person that you haven't thought about before?

See the wisdom in such forethought? I hope you do. I know a number of individuals who are trying to think in such a manner so that they can leave others well aware of their love and memory in a happy, comforting kind of way.

It is important in this kind of exercise to make notes afterward and to act upon some of the impressions you get. This stimulates the inner nature to remind you of other affairs to put in order, and other people who love and care about you who need a remembrance. One lady I know made out Christmas cards to some number of her friends including a "last" note. She wanted to say she cared one more time and this was the way she did it, leaving the cards to be mailed on the Christmas after her death.

Do not think this is an exercise just for those who are informed about a terminal illness. It is equally meaningful to everyone for the awareness it brings of the hole left in the lives of others when you withdraw. Think of a drill corps with one dropping out and the adjustment required by the rest to close the ranks. We all touch more lives than we know. Sudden death is very much like this, but any major change does much the same. Just think of the loneliness often brought on when a family, near and dear, moves to another residence or city. Change hurts. By making an effort such as this exercise, we are becoming more aware of our interlocking ties and we will always honor them with new respect as a result. We can dedicate ourselves to being more in touch and up-to-date from now on.

15

The Power of Touch

"The fears of dying belong to the body. The spirit does not carry the fear."

Recently I worked with a gentleman who suffered amyotrophic lateral sclerosis, more commonly called Lou Gehrig Syndrome or ALS. This slowly advancing condition brings death through deteriorating muscles as the patient gradually loses all capacity for movement. The physical body refuses any activation from the consciousness within; the personality is, in fact, the prisoner of the body.

This is one of the clearest examples we have of the difference between the body and consciousness. Also, I feel this can help us see that the thinking, indwelling spirit is truly not the body, but the user of the body.

In this extreme, diseased condition, the mind of the person is lucid, intelligent, functioning, while the body is unusable and is dying. The prisoner within awaits the point of death as a captive, knowing that in time the breath ends, vital functions fail ... and the body loses its hold on the spirit. I think this is an obvious demonstration that our spirit and body are merely working together for a time.

In our lifetime, most of us will have the opportunity to observe someone whose mind is very clear as his body is dying; or the reverse, we will see perfect physical bodies with the mental faculty gone. These illustrations help us realize that our physical, emotional, mental, and spiritual natures do not always cooperate. We then perceive more clearly that life, especially a constructive life, depends on a balance of these components.

I think of my friend who had ALS, and of his struggle as a consciousness within a cocoon-like body. The death of the body ended its grip on the spirit within. The consciousness escaped the body and began its life in spirit.

I had a dream one night about a year ago. It came to me long after I had been counseling in this field and I felt I had worked through my own fears of death. I had had the near-death experience of which I have written and was quite content within myself in this regard, or so I thought.

In the dream, a teacher I love and respect came to me and showed me a symbol, saying that when this sign occurs, I'd know I was dying. The particular sign came to pass (in the dream) and I recognized it. I, having complete trust in the teacher, accepted the validity of the sign and acknowledged that death was imminent.

I awoke frozen stiff, realized it was a dream, and lay there evaluating the situation. My breathing was rapid, my body was rigid, my heart was pounding. I got out of bed, thinking about the dream. I thought about my life — was this a warning? I thought hard about what was most important to me at this particular time. Finally I went back to bed.

Since then I have given consideration to this dream a number of times. I believe that our dreams come to us from our basic, subconscious nature, and that all of us are connected through a collective unconscious. We call it humanity, or the human qualities we share. The physical body is of this humanness. It is our vehicle of expression on the physical dimension and it is, in fact, terminal. The body does die and the fears of dying belong to the body and the physical part of our nature. The spirit, the soul, the next-dimensional inhabiter of the body, knowing that it continues to exist, does not carry the fear. As we know ourselves best in the physical state, we are more in touch with the outer, physical nature of ourselves than the inner essence. In one sense, we might say we instinctively know the fear because we know the body. In the same way, we know the need for food, sex, comfort, security.

If we can know the essence of our inner self as well as we know the external self, we are getting somewhere. We begin to recognize what part dies, what part doesn't. I think of a beautiful automobile and our attachment to it while it is new; but as years pass, we gradually appreciate it more for its usefulness. As the natural sequence of events will unfold, we'll again get excited, happy, and proud of another vehicle. The soul in its wisdom, knows the body is needed, appreciates and uses it, but knows it serves a function. The body can be realized as a functioning part; the spirit can be realized as a separate intelligence. This is the greatest value of "out-of-body" or "near-death" experiences. They reveal to an individual that there is a true ability to function separately. I think the lesson is to fully realize that we are not a body with a spirit, but instead, a spirit with a body. Knowing this, we, the spirit, can drop the body and find our immortality; also, we will recognize the mortality of the body without becoming defeated.

As people reach this level of understanding, they will be in a position to share with others. A remark often heard today is "I'd like to help but I don't know how." There is the recognition that dying ones need intelligent, loving support. This is why books such as this are being written, lectures given, and so many ideas and suggestions are being made. If there is a hospice or death and dying counselor in your area, call and ask questions. There are several spiritual groups and churches with death and dying discussion formats. In addition, colleges and universities can help you contact similar groups in your area. This book gives the new vision: You can do it. The key is feeling the inner desire to help the next person in the way that you recognize you need someone; become that kind of friend. This means a willingness to share the hurt so no one else feels the rejection and loneliness you have felt, or that you have seen in the lives of others. It means a willingness to share new perceptions about the indwelling spirit and the body vehicle.

A suggestion I have, if you are a support person to someone who has been told they are dying, or even if they just suspect it, is to use a lot of touching. Just as an infant can be reached through the subconscious and made secure by rocking or holding, so can adults. Taking walks, holding hands, sitting close; remember, as much touching as possible! Put the attention on just being there within reach, and wait for the timing which signals it's time to talk. There is no formula except to be natural. Statements like, "I really don't know either, but I'll be here," "We'll ask about that," and "I care and we'll manage," become strong building blocks. They are truths, not flowery promises, and this openness and honesty is felt and gives comfort. This is equally as true with children as with adults. The aware support person looks straight into the eyes of the suffering one and says, "I care. I'm here, let me help. I don't have to do anything, nor do you; I'll sit here. I can stand to hear you cry. I'll hold you in my arms or dry your tears. I've felt it, too."

In the supporting role, just as touch is a major comfort for one approaching death, massage, a form of touch, can be of primary aid to the survivor.

Massage is helpful in cases of sudden death or suicide. In the anguish of the situation, it is almost impossible for the bereaved to relax. Almost always the first hours of shock are so unacceptable, the survivor agonizes to the extent that sleep is impossible. Only in rare situations should medication be given.

While these hours are extremely difficult, coming to terms with death in our own way is critical at this point. Much therapeutic help is often required later if this period is blocked. Supportive friends need to be a part of these hours and there is little one can do except care and listen. The grief has to come out or great damage will be done. We need some ideas to guide us in this area.

Some time ago, I found that giving a massage works wonders. The touching and caressing of the physical body does help relax the nerves some, but much more important is the sense of security achieved by the touching.

We all need to be held, rocked, caressed, and told in no uncertain language that others care.

Massage is a way that works if we, ourselves, can be comfortable with this much touching. I have found a technique that seems to be a healing touch. One does not need much professional skill to give a helpful massage. To develop confidence, I recommend a massage workshop. Get the bereaved person you are working with to strip to underclothing and put him or her to bed, face-up, covered with a top sheet.

Start with the shoulders, arms and hands. Use some lotion or, if not available, simple vegetable oil from the kitchen. Gradually work out the tension of the muscles of one side, then the other. I touch and care, and I do little or no talking. Nearly always, the patient will cry and talk to you. This is excellent. The talking is therapeutic. An occasional, "yes," "Is that so?" or other non-judgmental comment keeps the stream of release flowing. After the arms and legs are done, I ask the person to turn over and work heavily on the back, which is the area where we carry responsibility, and then down the back of the legs.

All of this is done slowly and repeatedly. The goal is not to get finished, but to keep them releasing their grief as much and as long as possible. It is not unusual for me to spend one to one-and-a-half hours there. By the time this is done, a great deal has been accomplished.

Finishing, gently massage the face. Tenderly and quietly conclude the treatment. In some psychological way you are now rebuilding; getting this one ready to face the world again.

Even if they can't sleep now, you have been intimately involved with them during a most traumatic period and you've stayed with them supportively. They are well aware of your caring and this is desperately needed in shock situations.

For coping with the shock of sudden rejection, such as a loved one disappearing deliberately or committing suicide, massage is invaluable. These experiences leave such indelible scars on the psyche that as support persons, we want to render whatever immediate first-aid we can.

The bitter rejection experience often causes individuals to feel sexually inadequate and/or emotionally insecure for years to come. It is not uncommon for this type of experience to lead the survivor to pursue one lover after another, trying to deny the rejection and prove acceptability. We are in a unique place if we can be of immediate service and prevent some of this damage.

Similarly, the suicide of a loved one chills our heart so badly, we freeze with fear. Never knowing when love will be withdrawn again, we become afraid to love and block the very flowing force that could heal our life. An attitude of "I'll never place myself in such a vulnerable position again!" is quite common. Such lonely people lead dead lives, guilt-ridden, fearful of each day, berating themselves for their own immature, past actions or even for the actions of others. Therefore, compassionate support is one of the most loving gifts we can give to one who suffers in this way. Find your technique, a way to openly express your caring so that you, too, may be a positive life force giver!

16

Coping Techniques

"By the ritual of focusing upon the presence of light in meditation, we begin shifting from outer to inner worlds."

M any ancient sacrificial customs, trips to the temple, rituals and tokens are seen as foolish today. I suggest that those rituals were of greater value than we realize. They helped people show love and appreciation, gave direction as to how to express grief, and provided a means for releasing the intense emotions surrounding a loss. In our new, modern, less traditional attitude, we must rebuild some of these tools that are needed for the releasing process. Rituals will work for us when we believe them; the faith we place in a technique gives it its potency. Rituals help us cope when our intellect is cutting in and out, as it does under the shock and strain of grief-filled times. The dynamics of the spiritual services of all faiths are designed to aid both those who have passed and those left behind.

Part of the present difficulty with traditional vs. non-traditional views is that as some people are awakened to new concepts, they assume the old ways to be valueless.

Since they have not yet constructed the next ritual or pattern to help in times of trauma, they are frustrated.

One contemporary approach being tried is meditation, a process of contacting the inner life. I describe it as touching in with our true source. Whether or not we know anything about spiritual life, this process happens to us spontaneously, through day-dreaming, at a deep level where we actually lose contact with the outer world. This touching in, often called meditation, has a comforting, restoring effect. We forget our cares, float free of daily life, and get many of the benefits similar to sleep from these relief periods.

When one learns meditation for psychological reasons, certain benefits occur. Biofeedback can monitor the psychological changes as they manifest at the physical level. The psyche also experiences something but these more subtle changes cannot be so easily demonstrated.

Both the Old and New Testaments of the Bible support ideas of "entering into the silence of the Lord." Eastern teaching, suggesting more inner work than outer display, provides many techniques we can incorporate. The mystical Jewish Kabbala and esoteric Christianity, using Christian Mystery School patterns, encourage meditation as one of the four major spiritual disciplines. The other three disciplines are contemplation, prayer, and adoration.

Meditation is touching into the God Force within, or as may be more commonly expressed, contacting the Holy Spirit. This silent, inner experience is to strengthen us and to increase the spiritual power or force in life so we become fortified by the Living Presence; the stream of life itself.

While there are many meditative approaches taught, the most helpful in regard to death is the idea of following the light within. Light, symbolic of inspiration, wisdom, and intelligence, becomes the symbol of the Life Presence without form. The practice of picturing light filling the mind, head, and body, magnifies our oneness with the flow of life. It is taught that we can attach our consciousness to the stream of life. Flooding our being with light, surrendering to it, becomes a way to flow with life, whether we are in a physical body or have recently left it. By the ritual of focusing upon the presence of light in meditation, we begin the process of shifting from outer to inner worlds. Therefore, today many people are learning to meditate in preparation for the death transition as they move from the physical to spiritual worlds.

An expression repeatedly used in all spiritual teachings in regards to meditation is to "follow the light." Many visualize a white light to represent the formless God of the Universe, the Creative Source. Others find their minds fill with an inner light as they reach a deep, inner contact point. Most traditions use some form of the word "light" to represent the guiding presence of God. With our contemporary insight into this tradition, we have a new discovery which is called the Light Being: a novel idea, yet undoubtedly the very basic experience of countless numbers before us.

The great reason we are taught to follow the light or go to the light at death is for safe passage through the astral dimension or the emotional plane. If you've never heard these words before they can sound foreboding, but the ideas can be comforting and a bit of knowledge about this can be helpful.

A part of the physical world consists of a less dense, less solid dimension sometimes described as a shadow of the physical plane. This level overlaps the physical and accounts for the appearance of loved ones after death, and even the accounts of ghosts that we hear of from time to time.

This astral plane is made up of those people in transition who are more in touch with the dense, physical world than with the spirit level and those not wanting to move on for whatever reason. Often, for example, a young mother might lag behind to look after her child. An older mate might wait here for a partner for many years. A great many human traits affect us for some time after the immediate passing of the physical body. This is especially so if we have great emotional concerns or unfinished business on earth.

Several ancient traditions have written extensively about this process; probably the best known treatises are *The Egyptian Book of the Dead* and *The Tibetan Book of the Dead.* The two are considerably alike; they are difficult and of little help without esoteric understanding. However, if properly studied, they serve to acquaint us with other cultures which had more understanding about death than we do. There are great similarities between the near-death experiences of today and the ancient writings. As we share and experiment with meditation and inner work, the meaning of the material becomes clearer to us.

There is an exercise that is recommended to those who wish to grow spiritually as they understand more and more of the wisdom passed to us from the ancient Truths. It is called the daily review and in this practice you set aside a few minutes each evening and think back about the entire day.

You review the events of the day *backwards,* allowing each event or experience to be weighed on its own merits. When events are reviewed chronologically, they tend to run together, with the emotion of each incident pouring into the next as they do in the sequence of life. By going over them backward, one must divide the events into segments, breaking that sequence, thus requiring each occurrence to stand on its own merit. This causes one to recognize the energy or focus which started the event, your own contribution to the build-up of positive or negative energy, and your response.

When you find a situation in which you wish you had responded differently, there is additional action that can be taken:

You can think how you wish you had handled the situation. For example, wishing you had responded lovingly instead of with hostility to unkind remarks. You can, in fact, in mind and with mind, recreate the situation and act out in the mind a changed sequence of responses: See yourself keeping calm, staying centered, and responding gently, quietly, or even lovingly. This retake of the situation, while done inwardly, is actually helping to re-program, helping us learn to respond in a manner of our own choosing.

It's much like practicing your part in a play until you know the lines perfectly. In the review you are able to hold your emotional nature clear, to respond lovingly, and without explosion, you allow a triggering point to pass. The name of the game is to deal with the incident to your satisfaction. You gradually learn to conquer disturbing actions and the underlying emotions as well.

In addition, if we believe thoughts are things and if we can damage one another by hate-charged emotion or anger we direct toward each other, then we can spiritually attempt to make amends through this exercise. In the review, since we are now calm and working from the spiritual level of ourself, we can attempt to balance the destructive actions. In a loving way we can send forth thoughts of forgiveness, we can appreciate that other soul and its particular struggle, and we can send a stream of loving energy from us, accepting responsibility for our actions and our responses to others. We really begin to *be* the loving one. Spiritual students seeking to live a divine life get much assistance from this exercise. It requires daily thought about how we each respond to life. If we accept and release our responses, we can begin to be what we want to be.

This daily review is of great value when we begin to think of dying and the life review. Stories of life reviews are told by many who experience near-death. Reference is often made to near-drowning experiences when "My whole life flashed before me." Dr. George Ritchie's experience, described in Jon Mundy's book *Learning To Die,* is certainly an example. There are also biblical references to a judgment day after or in conjunction with death. In the esoteric tradition the belief is held that the Christ Within views the life and judges it and helps the personality to learn from its experience. Thus, students in the daily review seek to correct and upgrade their everyday life by continually trying to review their experiences from a spiritual level. In this manner it is possible to balance from the life level, rather than from a spirit level after death. It is believed this pattern speeds up the evolution of the soul, awakens spiritual qualities within, and produces a more spiritual personality, thus realizing the goal of a disciple of divine life.

I would like to apprise you here of another new technique which may become a ritual, a spiritual tradition, in our time: the inception of crying rooms in hospitals. This includes a psychotherapy approach of mourning, crying, screaming, and grieving openly which is a process rapidly building favor among those who have direct contact with bereaved people. Getting it all out as soon as possible sets so much healing into motion. It is one of the blessings of this new approach. Now that sex can be openly acknowledged, perhaps death can be looked upon as equally natural.

A young psychologist involved in Death Awareness Counseling in the Cincinnati area told me that if she lost a close friend or a family member, she would immediately enter a grief recovery group or go for private counseling, another modern approach which is becoming more and more acceptable. In her opinion, this is today's best way of getting through the re-balancing process so one can again pick up the business of living. I support this idea in theory but I want our society to adopt an approach which goes a step further.

We should not place the burden upon an individual to seek out such aid, but we should create an holistic approach to death. I envision a process of interlocking lives so that dying is done at home with the family.

Hospitals and nursing homes are needed and serve well in some situations, but even here we could find ways to humanize the situation. Much change and creativity must occur for these urine-saturated, drugged atmospheres to be converted to loving places within which anyone might want to live or die. A new breed of caring people is awakening to these sensitive situations and through the discontent being stirred up and the new ideas being inspired, I expect much change.

One change which is fairly new to the American scene is the hospice. Eagerly accepted by most, the hospice concept is designed for the care of the terminally ill. The foremost goal is to help the patient remain at home until death among the familiar setting and loved ones. In some areas the hospice actually has a facility purposely constructed to create an informal place for patients to be well cared for while encouraging pets, children and friends to share this time. The hospice idea suggests one be allowed his last desires as much as possible. A great deal of effort is made to prepare each person in the family as well as close friends for the end of life by helping each one live positively day-by-day and hour-by-hour.

Hospices, new to most of us, are introducing natural methods of love and caring to the fearful experience of death. There is a great realization that there's more to death than the clinical aspect. A strong interest in the whole family's participation makes for an atmosphere of support and integrates death into the wholeness of life.

In hospices, volunteers are trained to work with doctors, nurses, social workers and spiritual counselors. Volunteers are accepted from every walk of life. A sincere desire to help is as important as any credential. Persons having experienced loss usually are of the greatest benefit to others facing the experience. Each day is allowed to unfold without a hospital atmosphere. In most cities, as of yet, the movement consists of an office, some trained and dedicated professionals, and a large number of loving and helpful adventurous people.

The strength of the movement has grown from the generosity of the dedicated workers. The hospice idea is meeting a need in the lives of the patients, yes, but equally so in our society. A new way of facing death is being sought. I expect us to see many variations on this idea in the immediate future.

As you can well surmise from these remarks, I am totally in support of the hospice movement. I believe in addition, from a practical point of view, that much of the high cost of medical care can thus be circumvented. If we begin now to become involved in the whole process of care and death, we can expect a better future for ourselves and our children.

Individuals who may be involved with a dying patient professionally and/or personally are all support persons. We automatically think of friends and family, but we must extend that picture to include the professionals giving attention and advice. Also, professionals must be helped to know it is expected and acceptable for them to give some sincere caring from their personal selves. Otherwise, we might as well cease referring to this group as the "caring profession." This list certainly includes doctors and nurses, but also includes attorneys, bankers, ministers, priests, rabbis, social workers, physical therapists, and emergency assistants. Last, but by no means least, we must include funeral home directors and crematory specialists who have needed skills. All these occupations have grown out of the human need. In becoming capable, professionals often become cool and detached. Most of the cool detachment is a form of self-protection, a way for them to avoid getting involved; perhaps because they feel they have no real answer.

Believe me, there *is* a real answer: Share the experience! Speak of it honestly, admit you can do little but care, but do your caring openly. Let the patient hear you say, "I am sharing your experience. I am here." In this framework, they get permission to be totally honest, to be real. There is the freedom to think out loud, cry, ask someone to sit awhile and tarry with them on this day. If professionals can be intimately connected to the situation, then the family members, friends, and even the patient get a model for the roles needed to develop a real support system, even if there is no monumental solution. Our nature is such that we do mimic one another. We follow the pattern of those we admire, and at this time in our society, professionals are highly respected. As support persons, professional and personal, the new call is to *care* as we share; freely, honestly, and openly.

17

Rituals of Passage

"I do not fear death itself as much as the indignities of deterioration, dependence and hopeless pain."

— *The Living Will*

We can hardly explore the many aspects of the closing stages of life, the question of continuing life, and the assistance necessary for those involved in the death process, without moving naturally into the subject of funerals and memorial services.

At a point when social traditions are rapidly changing, some feel compelled to follow the custom of religion or family tradition. Others, repelled by rituals or customs which seem sterile or uncaring, cry out for a new way to deal with such a tender time.

I think it is important to remember all that we have previously said about style as we try to find the way that will work best for us. People have their own styles, their own personal mannerisms.

I have heard crude remarks made about fashionable masses for Mafia members by those who have stereotyped pictures of persons, wealthy and supposedly unethical, receiving a most Christian burial; the life style and service seemingly in opposition. Sometimes political and business persons known to be unethical are eulogized in glowing terms when they are gone. For these and other reasons, much of society is reaching a point of resisting traditional funeral arrangements (I disagree with this leap of logic). Today, the public is reaching for some answers that can meet more appropriately an up-to-date code.

We are realizing that to be consistent and true, a funeral must suit a person just as his clothing and home do. Because the home is more or less a good reflection of the individual, I often support a memorial service in this setting.

If a person is a regular temple or church-goer, yes, his service probably will be most fitting there. That worship participation has been vital to the life and the ritual will be an appropriate salutation of the life. However, if the deceased has not been actively engaged in religious worship, has not participated in years or perhaps was never inclined that way, why not recognize the life for what it did value?

New approaches can be and are developed to replace outgrown or unused ritual. One of the most natural, comfortable, and sincere is the home memorial service. At this time, more and more people are breaking with tradition in order to have a service of deep, personal meaning for themselves. The home memorial is a gathering of close friends and family to celebrate the life of the deceased. Each service differs, but an air of informality is the rule. A minister may speak and/or guide the service, with close friends and members of the family taking part. Often there is a reading of some of the thoughts of the deceased or original or favorite poetry is selected. Children may read a poem, sing a song, or express their thoughts. This is a time for a loving bon voyage for the departed. There may or may not be food afterward. More and more there is an emphasis placed upon picking up the pieces and going forward, recognizing the good that has come to each life through its contact with the departed person. Pictures are often displayed and there is a definite feeling established of closing one door and opening the next. Thus, the human need for helpful ritual at changing point is fulfilled. Often, as I see these healing, loving times, I think of the passage in Ecclesiastes declaring the day of death being better than the day of birth. Only now are we beginning to deal with the wisdom those words contain.

Memorial services must be arranged sensitively, according to the family and situation. It is to be as personal as you care to make it according to the tender feelings of the group involved. Avoid detachment, formality, and triteness. The idea is to build a safe place of deep love to help in healing the grief of those left behind. This healing force comforts and encourages new life to flow and while it is the send-off for the deceased, it is also a major turning point for survivors. The healing force aids them to let go of the past and begin to think of the changes ahead. These services are needed to help us have a feeling of completeness and of turning a corner to the next segment of life. We do not need to do away with the tradition of funerals and memorial services; we need to learn to use them in a more constructive way.

These rituals are indeed painful because they remind us so much of our own vulnerability. Intellectually, we all know our days are numbered, but we do not wish to be reminded. When one close to us disappears behind that veil, we react from a deep and vulnerable place within our nature. The more natural life and death, or the idea of continuing life, becomes to us, the less trauma we will encounter. The less we experience this kind of trauma, the more naturally we respond to others in their varying situations and the better support people we become.

Suppose you are not ready for such a home memorial service yet. Consider an informal church service. It's harder to be informal in that setting, but certain things can be done. Several friends can speak and if the music is changed, and the words "celebration of life" are used, some barriers naturally come down. Family attitude is the major factor. Greeting friends warmly rather than withdrawing indicates a new understanding of the situation. In this setting, reading favorite poems, perhaps original pieces by the deceased or the family, is really effective. Speaking of the person in a close and personal way with a sincere manner rather than the euphemistic eulogies of the past makes the difference. Clothing needs to be less formal, brighter, more natural.

Sometimes an informal gathering can be held in a park, at a lovely beach or in the yard or garden, if such is possible. Think of this, especially for one who loved nature. Do not feel you are locked into any arrangement. You are expressing your love and appreciation for this person's contribution to your life and structuring a setting in which others may feel your love and express theirs.

Your style is your particular way of expressing a nature which is unique to you. My style is the manner I use in writing this book, my personal insights and reactions to life, the combination that has the stamp of "Carol" on it for me. Your style rings true for you. My words represent me; yours carry your personal resonance of truth. Everyone is made up of their own special realities, arrived at in their own experience. That combination of realities, mannerisms, energies, and insights is clothed in the way you think, dress, talk, and react to events. Your approach to pain and confusion, joy and happiness, new people and events, change and death should reflect your unique personality. Sometimes a shock sweeps you out of your style for a bit, but as you re-balance, individuality should return. If we don't like something about our particular style, we have to eliminate a quality, a fault, or an approach through the cultivation of something more preferable.

Energy moves and cuts little rivulets in the brain called patterns, or habits. These patterns, once embedded, are not easily changed, but they can be altered by effort or modification of the patterns. Since the style of each person is made up of the accumulation of a life's perspective, change usually comes slowly and only with patience and hard work.

There was a story in the news some time ago about a man's family who gathered around him in his last hours, sang all his favorite songs and played guitar, sharing his final time in this way. Because this man was famous, it made the news, but many such experiences are occurring throughout the world.

Do not overlook the idea that tradition still plays an important role in many people's lives. If it has been helpful and important to some in the past, it will help now. Be aware of what is meaningful both to you and to the deceased. To be of help, many who plan ahead talk about their own memorial service, discussing and planning with mates or family. This is, of course, the very best way. It takes a safe, loving, support system for a dying person to openly discuss such plans. Don't expect everyone to be able to do it. The choice of burial or cremation should be discussed, as it can be terribly difficult for family members to decide after the death. If an individual feels strongly one way or the other, it should be known and respected. If it matters little, be sensitive to the mate and then the children. Be gentle in exploring ideas together for each idea may be wrought with fear. As the discussion progresses, emotion is everywhere. Each one should be gentle and sensitive, knowing this to be delicate work, touching subconscious ideas, fears, memories, and bringing the long, un-faced pains forward, now to be dealt with.

By virtue of their profession, ministers have had to deal with such matters as these, but it does not mean they deal with them well. Often they are most guilty of a professionalism that is permeated by their personal denial to face their own suppressed feelings. Death and dying counselors are the ones most prepared to be of help here. They have usually faced their own pain and have dared to be vulnerable or they wouldn't be in this particular field.

Individuals who staff funeral homes and/or crematories are in a unique situation. Their role can involve manipulation thriving on emotionalism and pain, or be one of great service. The opportunity to serve those in pain, grief, and often shock, is unique and can be a high, ethical service. Not everyone in these professions can rise to the desired level of performance, of course. There certainly is, in our society at this time, a need for workers in these fields to have great sensitivity and become aware of the need for change. Since these workers can be great support persons for the survivors of any death situation, it is important that they be inspired and dedicated individuals.

Aware persons, supportive and loving, will examine these suggestions for a newer approach to funerals and memorial services. Let us hope that they will be incorporated into a meaningful modern tradition.

The hospice concept suggests one be allowed his last desires as much as possible. Elisabeth Kübler-Ross tells of deaths which have included wine and candlelight. Children can be held tenderly or pets curled up at the foot of the bed.

Some of these ideas seem strange when we first hear of them; they are so new. But which would we choose: to be drugged out of consciousness in a hospital or to be free of drugs or only slightly medicated (an advantage of a hospice), and if at all possible, to have every last moment together?

Realize also that these new ideas make life much more guilt-free for families. They can participate in the life of the loved one to the last, especially in a home atmosphere and relaxed setting rather than in a strange corridor or limited visiting plan which excludes beloved children and pets.

I have encouraged home care whenever possible, with family and friends participating in the real life drama of death. We all need to be part of Life and Death in order to prepare for our own turn. I suggest singing to the dying one, or reading and writing poetry. Never mind that he or she cannot respond. The spirit is conscious and knows and wants you near. Read letters from friends, tell the news of others and *touch*.

Several times I've advised gentle, ever so gentle, washing or massage with lotion over the body in the last hours. If there is no pain at touch, this is most comforting. Even if the person cannot respond, if you know there isn't pain, gently rub or stroke with lotion. Stroke, hum, sing, visit, play the favorite tunes. Write letters to others and read them aloud, ever mindful that you're being a best friend, a support person all the way.

If you are questioning the degree of medication the patient should have to keep comfortable, inquire through your physician or the local hospice about the Brampton mixture. Elisabeth Kübler-Ross writes, "With the help of G. Humma, a pharmacist at the Indianapolis Methodist Hospital, a handbook of the Brampton mixture was developed and became available to any physician who was willing to try this marvelous cocktail and who was encouraged to send patients home to die without the need for injections and frequent medical supervision."

I don't believe this book would be complete without a reference to a document commonly called *The Living Will*. An example is shown on the following page:

To my family, physician, lawyer, clergyman
To any medical facility in whose care I happen to be
To any individual who may become responsible for my
health, welfare or affairs:

Death is as much a reality as birth, growth, maturity and old age — it is the one certainty of life. If the time comes when I, _____, can no longer take part in decisions for my own future, let this statement stand as an expression of my wishes, while I am still of sound mind.

If the situation should arise in which there is no reasonable expectation of my recovery from physical or mental disability, I request that I be allowed to die and not be kept alive by artificial means or "heroic measures." I do not fear death itself as much as the indignities of deterioration, dependence and hopeless pain. I therefore ask that medication be mercifully administered to me to alleviate suffering even though this may hasten the moment of death.

This request is made after careful consideration. I hope you who care for me will feel morally bound to follow its mandate. I recognize that this appears to place a heavy responsibility upon you, but it is with the intention of relieving you of such responsibility and of placing it upon myself in accordance with my strong convictions, that this statement is made.

Signed _____

Date _____

Witness _____

Witness _____

This type of request is growing in popularity and anyone can prepare such a document, have it witnessed and added to his or her legal papers. It certainly serves to help professionals and family know the strong feelings of the signer. Such a decision is extremely hard for a family to come to in the midst of a crisis. Often any talk of taking a person off a support system invokes great guilt in parties involved despite whatever strong, logical arguments may prevail.

Yes, it's a courageous time of change that we live in. Dying at home, surrounded by loved ones and pets, with someone reading poetry or singing favorite songs in the light of candles or with the sunshine streaming through a window, certainly has a lot going for it. Let's try it!

18

Continuing Life

"What has been set into motion by the great creative Source of life continues."

The challenge of our time is not to debate right or wrong, traditional versus non-traditional. It is to accept death, inevitable for all of us, as a part of life, then incorporate it and its preparatory stages into living. We begin by playing with new and varying ideas, and as we can, use them as we deal with the occasions presented to us. For many at this time, just talking openly about the subject is a big step forward. There is a great relief when that happens and the dying one and the survivor can openly discuss that which presses closely upon the mind and heart of each.

It's difficult to understand how Christian ministers could speak out against such works as Dr. Raymond Moody's *Life After Life*. This work relies on the newest scientific efforts possible to report a recurring experience that points to an after-world, and every Christian minister has mentioned an afterlife since the words came from Jesus' lips. Another powerful scientific investigation of near-death experiences is a book called *Life at Death* by

Kenneth Ring. He seeks to look in an objective manner at the experiences of after-life.

What is it that keeps Christians from standing in one accord, celebrating this great step in research? My feeling is that it is because there is no clear-cut heaven/hell issue in these books. If half the revived or resuscitated individuals had come back describing the pain of hell-fire and the other half had come back exclaiming over harps and music, many ministers would have rejoiced, for this has been the traditional message. As it is, because there is no misgiving in the information we've gotten from these revived people, the fear of God isn't evident nor are people inclined to seek out the Church to help them "change their ways." For this reason, the evidence seems contrary to those preaching eternal life. Maybe more than ever the loving Beings encountered by so many are trying to show us God is much more loving than we are; I certainly hope so.

As we work with dying individuals, we find there are many new ways to handle unfinished business. I think of a most proper, loving father who held much anger in his heart regarding a daughter who had not lived up to his expectations. She was living with a young man, they were not married, and he considered this a great sin. He had disinherited her, he wouldn't allow her name to be spoken in his presence, and he dealt with the matter as if she no longer existed.

In his last days, I brought this up, making reference to unfinished business. He didn't want to discuss it, feeling totally justified in his stand. I told him I was terribly sorry for his daughter and was shocked at his cruelty. I called to his attention that he was, in fact, condemning her to live with his disapproval the rest of her life. As long as she lived, she would remember him with feelings of condemnation and separation. All her memories of the loving father of her childhood would be clouded with his disapproval. If and when she changed her life style, begged forgiveness, suffered, whatever it was he would have for her, how could he then let her know she was forgiven? Could he not say to her now, "I love you, even though I do not approve of your actions"?

Before his death a few weeks later, he called his daughter on the telephone. Though he couldn't change his mind about his disapproval of her life style, he told her he loved her. By the time he died, he and his daughter were assured of the continuance of their loving relationship.

We all need to ask ourselves if we should carry our hostility and condemnation for others to our end. Or should this be the time, as we contemplate with new awareness the biblical words, "forgive us our debts, as we forgive our debtors," that we let go of earthly matters, loving and forgiving, so that we can go on about the business of spiritual growth and allow those we forgive to continue to grow and change according to the spiritual self within them.

Death must be faced whether a person is spiritually inclined or not. Perhaps ministers can help spiritual people according to their own denominations; this has been the supposition. However, when Dr. Kübler-Ross challenges groups, including ministers, to say that they really do believe in a next stage of life, few accept the challenge.

My sharing is meant to be just that, a sharing of experiences that serve as material for individuals to think about. I *know* a form of life continues and this I would share to give comfort and new hope to many who do not know.

I feel life continues and not in the clear-cut heaven and hell, Judeo-Christian concepts. I believe that in the Father's house there are many mansions and we know very little about them.

I think the whole history of art, drama, inspired thought, and mythology offers us ideas about angels and a spirit world. The biblical references are certainly frequent; the Hindus make reference to the devas; the Hebrews have the Netherland and its inhabitants; the ancient Egyptians had Tuat, the common name for the abode of the departed, and throughout time individuals have told their ghost stories. Unusual phenomena, however frightening at times, intrigue and attract us because we do not comprehend the how's and why's of another dimension. I think that many clues to Truth are hidden in the most obvious places, in everyday life, waiting for our need or our desire to find them.

If we can still sense the spirit of ancient Egypt in the King Tut exhibit or feel the power of an absent artist in his work, why can't we believe in the spirit of an individual continuing?

I am convinced that what has been set into motion by the great creative Source of life continues. The law of physics states that energy only changes form; it cannot be destroyed. I believe, emphatically, in life here and there, onward and upward, linking together a chain of humanity, our lives and souls intertwined. Whether we know or hope or care, humanity moves forward, made in the image and likeness of the intelligence of the All.

We come to *know* death as a friend.

LET THERE BE PEACE

Epilogue

If I had to write this book today, I couldn't. This week I buried my twenty-two-year-old daughter and her two-year-old child. Mary Beth and Alexis lost their lives in a one-car automobile accident. Alexis was asleep in her father's lap as he drove the family home late in the evening. The day had been good; he and Mary had enjoyed themselves.

The peculiar chain of events began when Alexis awakened and pulled herself up, using the steering wheel. The unexpected pull flipped the truck sideways just as the vehicle crossed a narrow bridge with no railing. The fashionable Florida subdivision had dug channels to create water-front lots. The channel beneath them was twelve feet deep. Twenty minutes later, Mary Beth's body was pulled from the water. It is believed the blow to the right side of her head had knocked her unconscious; she was pronounced dead on arrival at the Community Hospital. The paramedics worked feverishly to resuscitate the baby pulled from the vehicle. Her heart started. After being rushed to the small, local hospital for emergency assistance, she was transferred by ambulance to Pediatrics Intensive Care at Tampa General Hospital for the finest care possible. Sixty hours later, she joined her mother in death. Realizing she was severely brain-damaged, we watched the beautiful body complete its effort to survive and came to understand, from personal experience, the struggle of wanting life to continue yet aware of the healing that death often brings.

On Friday, Mary Beth and Alexis were laid to rest together. My heart is touched by the love and gentleness of many persons. Again, I had seen first hand the drama of death. Coming home, I picked up the manuscript of this book to reread it and to see if my words, echoing back to me, could stand the test of my experience. I find the words ring true and I am including some additional insights here as well.

ﻌ   ﻌ   ﻌ

Touching the body, hair or hand of the deceased helps us to deal with the reality and finality of their physical life. Just as long ago families dealt with life and death close-up — having births at home, self-doctoring their wounds, and washing and dressing the bodies of their own deceased — we are again beginning to participate in these previously unmentionable experiences. Participation in the total life experience makes us holistically well beings.

More and more we are realizing we need to be fully conscious, un-drugged, facing birth with its joy and its pain, with our love flowing. By fully embracing and accepting our bodies, we bond together as families. Strengthening our ties to one another at these crisis points helps us to be responsible participants in our lives in the future. The multidimensional levels of each one of us use these opportunities to grow and to bond. If we allow as many crises as possible to be handled by professionals and outsiders, how do we find our true strength? In our avoidance of the pain, we usually miss one of life's most poignant moments. We need, as a people, to stop thinking someone else knows what to do better than we, ourselves. The professional can, of course, be a support person, but personal integrity, strength of character and stability are found through rising to the painful occasions life presents to us.

One of the most painful experiences of my encounters with death came when preparing for the funeral of my daughter. The task of selecting the casket and clothing was mine. The time came for selecting a shroud and there was no way I could let my fashion-conscious, lovely young woman wear the old-lady frocks on display. Most of her clothes were modern sun-dresses, and I simply couldn't go home to her closet and get something. I found myself in a mall shopping for a suitable outfit. Engaging that strength we all have, I "gritted my teeth" and just did it. I looked until I found a cowl-necked, cotton sweater like the ones I had given her for her last Christmas, and a lacy jumper she could have worn and enjoyed. It mattered a lot that she wore what was natural to Mary Beth.

To walk through the mall, a natural part of everyday, twentieth-century life, and select clothing for your dearly beloved deceased is a test of endurance. Only a heart brave, but also loving, can do this. As I looked at her wearing the garments later, I thought how pleased I felt. I had participated in preparing her in this way. I helped my levels-of-self integrate the past and present, and also found strength to help build my future.

I now struggle with the loss of my daughter and granddaughter. We call such happenings tragic accidents, yet there is a place in me that knows these events are part of the fabric of life. I am comforted in my loss, made certain by the knowledge of my own encounter with death; that gentle Being of Light we know by such a fearful name. I hold tightly to my own death experience as my conscious mind struggles to compute the reality of this new loss into my everyday life.

As the author of this book, I need to acknowledge how I find myself reacting to this occurrence. It amazed me to observe parts of myself dealing with the reality of this pain-filled event. I believe my struggle to integrate and comprehend the experience is the struggle every one of us shares. This is part of our oneness.

At times my head is in silent, unruffled, smooth peace. My mind computes, calculates, plans, realizes all the many details I must take care of. I think about gas for the car; messages to be telephoned to others; etc. Then, at times, even while the smooth flow of thought is in the foreground of my mind, I feel the stirring of a new wave of pain growing from another level. This pain advances upon me until it breaks my conscious line of thought and the rational mind loses its grasp for a brief respite — the wave of grief is followed by a second or two of relief — no thought — then memory re-invades and either tears flow or a deep breath restores the thinking process.

I believe this is the natural pattern of grief and repair. I feel the process happening within myself and capture it to study. The emotional nature feels like a deep ocean, the surface being the mental part of myself. When I'm observing, I know I am driving my car, answering questions, or making arrangements for flowers. Then, even as I am conscious of the sun shining or of the surface activity, another grieving part begins to feel the stirring, the working to the surface from the depths. The rolling wave has begun. From the slightest recall or recognition, word, or prompting, the motion begins to grow. I resist knowing the pain is on its way as long as I can, denying the surge coming to the foreground, not wanting to deal with it. It's like standing at the beach watching the waves come in. Useless to run screaming at the water ... "Stop! Stop! I've had enough!" Useless to fight the pain, for the waves are a part of life — not mine, nor yours, this pain belongs to Life.

This pain is Life's. So the mind stops and allows the wave to invade it, just as the dry beach sand accepts the water of the sea wetting its surface. The wisdom of the sand knows the tide will subside. This kind of grief subsides, not because we no longer care or eventually learn to cope, but because an expansion of consciousness occurs to help us truly know both living and dying are part of the natural process.

Look at the seashore: The water and the sand are naturally working, creating, and expressing together.

Dealing with my personal grief makes me acutely aware of the levels of myself which are interacting. How many of us are watching that process on any given day? There is the wise level, the philosophical part of our nature, that says, "Well, I believe so-and-so," or, "I *do* believe," or, "I know it." This part does know and is trying to support the actions of the other levels.

Another part doesn't know anything and doesn't even want to. This part just hurts. It doesn't care what the doctors say, or what the reasons or explanations are. This part needs to cry, to scream, to hit something! It bellows its scream of agony skyward.

Black and white these two parts are. Then there is the integration of the two, all the multitudinous shades of gray. The flash of insights, the incidents of recall, the happy memory of last Christmas, the sense of relief: "I'm so glad I did such and such," and the feelings of regret over the undone or unsaid, are weaving themselves together into one pattern; a pattern which forms our character. We are reacting out of previously developed habit patterns, spiritual strengths, expressive modes and energy levels of our being. We may find ourselves out of bed, walking the floor, because the energy level has gotten too high or tense. If we can release some of it, we can then go back to bed and perhaps to sleep.

People will also get up and unconsciously slip into habits of smoking, drinking coffee, saying the Rosary, or some similar religious ritual, cleaning out the cabinets, perhaps taking a walk around the block. These motions can all be done from the rote part of self. We are using an old performance to stabilize, because we *know* how to function in this mode, but we don't know yet how to *change* and react to these sudden necessary adjustments.

Gradually the new pattern is learned. As I try to think of my world without Mary Beth and the baby, I am acutely aware of the hole blown in the fabric of my existence; aware of the abrupt rupturing of my picture of her future and of my part interwoven into that future. Hopes explode in midair and plans jettison.

The wise level of self puts in a word or two, interjects great wisdom which my mother/grandmother personality doesn't want to hear. Mother/grandmother wants to say, "I can protect them. I deny this — I won't have it! Turn back the frames and let's replay this part of the movie. I demand a different script. This can't be so!"

The wise and knowing part, vastly in tune with life, brings its wisdom to mother/grandmother and says, "This is the stuff character is made of. You are a child of the Universe and you will experience what the Universe has to offer!"

Once life is conceived, it's entire rhythm is to be experienced. Breathe deeply; learn to flow with it. The great pain of your labor will be followed by the incredible beauty and joy of new life.

The age old wisdom comes to us from every direction. Yesterday I buried my daughter and grandchild. Happily, today a man tells me of the birth of a new child and I smile at him with love. He has thus assured me of the continuity of life. Yes, it is security at its most basic level. My pain didn't stop all life. Thank God that life is so huge; happiness and beauty are still out there taking place. I need that reassurance. Now I can cry the mote from my eye, knowing Beauty lives, knowing I *need* happy moments.

Resource Guide

When someone you love is dying, there is help for you in your community if you will reach out for it. You can start by calling your local Visiting Nurses Association or Hospice. Other local groups which can be of help are Churches, Synagogues, the Town Hall or City Hall, the Chamber of Commerce, the Hospital and the United Way.

The following organizations are sources of additional information and support.

GENERAL

California Medical Association
P.O. Box 7690, San Francisco, CA 94120
For information on the Durable Power of Attorney For Health Care and the Directive to Physicians.
(415) 541-0900

Center For Attitudinal Healing
Gerald Jampolsky
21 Main Street, Tiburon, CA   94920
(415) 435-1622

Center For Help In Time Of Loss
600 Blue Hill Rd., River Vale, NJ   07675
(201) 391-4473
Non-profit organization which holds grief recovery groups.

Concern for Dying
250 West 57th St., Suite 831, New York, NY 10019
212-246-6962
Source of information on the Living Will. Gives confer-ences and workshops throughout the country and prints a quarterly newsletter. Non-profit organization.

Elisabeth Kübler-Ross Center
S. Route 616, Headwaters, VA 24442
(703) 396-3441
National Headquarters. They will provide you with a list of Friends of Elisabeth Kübler-Ross *support groups throughout the United States and the world.*

Light of Christ Church
Reverend Carol Parrish-Harra
Sparrow Hawk Village
P.O. Box 1274, Tahlequa, OK 74464

Los Angeles Center For Living
1600 N. Sierra Bonita, Los Angeles, CA 90046
(213) 850-0877
(213) 850-0878
Non-profit agency providing walk-in services for the terminally ill and their families. Suppliers of Cassandra Christenson's wonderful audio tape A Guidance Through Death.

National Hospice Organization
1901 North Ft. Myer, Suite 307, Arlington, Virginia 22209
(703) 243-5900
Non-profit organization which provides free literature and can help you locate the hospice nearest you.

Progressive Nursing Services
8235 Santa Monica Blvd., Suite 211
West Hollywood, CA 90046
(213) 650-1800

AIDS

AIDS Project Los Angeles
3670 Wilshire Blvd., Suite 300, Los Angeles, CA 90010
(213) 380-2000
Non-profit organization providing support for AIDS patients in the Los Angeles area.

M.A.P. (Mothers of AIDS Patients)
P.O. Box 1763, Lomita, CA 90717
Provides information, group and individual counseling and a hotline service (numbers listed below) for families and loved ones of AIDS patients. Information on The PWA National AIDS Bracelet Program may be obtained here.

Joyce Brink	(213) 542-3019
Barbara Cleaver	(213) 530-2109
Helenclare Cox	(818) 794-1455
Mary Jane Edwards	(213) 541-3134
Janet McMahon	(213) 542-3019
Bea Simon	(213) 661-1954

Nechama - A Jewish Response To AIDS
"Nechama means comfort"
6000 West Pico Blvd., Los Angeles, CA 90035
(213) 934-2617

Shanti Project
890 Hayes St., San Francisco, CA 94117
(415) 558-9644
Support sevices of all kinds for AIDS patients and their loved ones.

GRIEF RECOVERY: CHILD LOSS

A.M.E.N.D.
Aiding Mothers & Fathers Experiencing Neo-Natal Death
Maureen Connelly
4324 Berrywick Terrace, St. Louis, MO 63128
(314) 487-7582
A support group and referral service for parents who have experienced miscarriage, stillbirth or loss of a newborn.

Compassionate Friends
P.O. Box 3696, Oak Brook, IL 60522
(312) 990-0010
Holds support groups throughout the U.S. for parents and siblings grieving the death of a child.

National Foundation for Sudden Infant Death
330 North Charles St., Baltimore, MD 21201
1-800-638-7437
Provides information on SIDS and referrals for clinical services and support groups in your area.

National Sudden Infant Death Syndrome Foundation
P.O. Box 2474, Landover Hills, MD 20784
1-800-221-7437

Parents of Murdered Children
100 East 8th St. , Suite B41, Cincinnati, OH 45202
(513) 721-5683 (office)
1-800-327-2499 ext. 4288 *for emergency counseling at any time. Support groups nationwide.*

S.H.A.R.E.
Source of Help in Airing and Resolving Experiences
St. John's Hospital, 800 E. Carpenter
Springfield, IL 62769
(217) 544-6464 ext. 5275
Counseling and referrals for parents coping with miscarriage, stillbirth or loss of a newborn.

GRIEF RECOVERY: WIDOWED PERSONS

Widowed Persons Service
1909 K Street NW, Washington, DC 20049
(202) 872-4700

Theos
717 Liberty , 1301 Clark Building, Pittsburgh, PA 15222
(412) 471-7779
This group has a spiritual emphasis and maintains 100 chapters nationwide.

SUICIDE

American Association of Suicidology
2459 South Ash, Denver, CO 80222
(303) 692-0985
They will provide you with a list of support groups in your area.

Survivors of Suicide
Sharry Schaefer
3251 N. 78th St., Milwaukee, WI 53222
(414) 442-4638
Counseling and referrals.

Students Against Suicide
P.O. Box 115, South Laguna, CA 92677
(714) 496-4566
Teenagers working to prevent teen suicide and provide support for teens and their families.

Suggested Readings

AIDS: A Self-Care Manual, AIDS Project Los Angeles. Santa Monica, California: IBS Press, 1987.*

The Bereaved Parent, Harriet Sarnoff Schiff. New York: Crown Books, 1977.

Birth to Birth, The Life Death Mystery, Rev. Gerald P. Ruane. New York: Alba House, 1976.

Children and Death, Elizabeth Kübler-Ross, M.D. New York: Macmillan, 1985.

A Course In Miracles, Tiburon, California: Foundation For Inner Peace, 1983.

Death and the Family, L. Pincus. New York: Pantheon Books, 1974.

Death Be Not Proud, John Gunther. New York: Harper & Row, 1949.

Death, The Final Stage of Growth, Elisabeth Kübler-Ross, M.D. Englewood Cliffs, New Jersey: Prentice-Hall, 1975.

Explaining Death to Children, Earl Grollman. Boston, Massachusetts: Beacon Press, 1967.

Gifts for the Living: Conversations With Caregivers On Death and Dying, BettyClare Moffatt. Santa Monica, California: IBS Press, 1988.*

Grief and How to Live with It, Sarah Morris. New York: Grosset and Dunlap, 1972.

How Do We Tell The Children? Dan Schaefer and Christine Lyons. New York: New Market Press, 1986.

Living With a Man Who Is Dying: A Personal Memoir, Jocelyn Evans. New York: Taplinger, 1971.

Living With Death and Dying, Elisabeth Kübler-Ross, M.D. New York: Macmillan, 1981.

Love Is Letting Go Of Fear, Gerald Jampolsky. New York: Bantam Books, 1981.

The Many Faces of Grief, Edgar N. Jackson. Nashville, Tennessee: Abingdon Press, 1972.

Questions On Death and Dying, Elisabeth Kübler-Ross. New York: MacMillan, 1974.

Someone You Love Is Dying (A Guide for Helping & Coping), Martin Shepard, M.D. New York: Harmony Books, 1975.

A Sorrow Beyond Dreams: A Life Story, Peter Handke. London: Souvenir Press, 1976.

Stepping Stones To Grief Recovery, Deborah Roth. Santa Monica, California: IBS Press, 1988.*

To Live Again: Rebuilding Your Life After You've Become A Widow, Genevieve Ginsburg; Los Angeles: Jeremy P. Tarcher, 1987*

Unconditional Love And Forgiveness, Edith Stauffer. Burbank, California: Triangle Publishers, 1987.*

When Someone You Love Has AIDS: A Book of Hope for Family and Friends, BettyClare Moffatt. New York: NAL Penguin, 1987.*

Widow, Lynne Caine. New York: Bantam Books, 1974.

*These books may be ordered directly from:

IBS Press
744 Pier Avenue
Santa Monica, CA 90405
(213) 450-6485

IBS Press also distributes the Durable Power of Attorney for Health Care and the Directive to Physicians (Living Will).

Bibliography

Bach, Richard. *Illusions, The Adventures of A Reluctant Messiah*.
New York: Delacorte Press, 1977.

Basset, Elizabeth. *The Bridge is Love: an anthology of hope*.
London: Darton, Longman and Todd, 1981

Budge, E.A. Wallis. *Egyptian Book Of The Dead*. New York:
Dover, 1967.

Evans-Wentz, W.Y. *The Tibetan Book Of The Dead*. New York:
Oxford University Press, 1960.

Feifel, Herman. *The Meaning Of Death*. New York: McGraw
Hill, 1977.

Hampton, Charles. *The Transition Called Death*. Wheaton, IL:
Theosophical Publishing House, 1979.

Hodson, Geoffrey. *Reincarnation, Fact Or Fallacy?* Wheaton, IL:
Theosophical Publishing House, 1967.

Holy Bible, King James Version.

Jackson, Edgar N. *Telling A Child About Death*. New York:
Channel Press, 1965.

Kübler-Ross, Elisabeth. *On Death And Dying*. New York:
MacMillan, 1974.

_____. *Death: The Final Stage of Growth*.
Englewood Cliffs, NJ: Prentice-Hall, 1975.

_____. *To Live Until We Say Goodbye*.
Englewood Cliffs, NJ: Prentice-Hall, 1978.

Lilly, John C. *The Center of the Cyclone*. New York: Bantam
Books, 1973.

Moody, Jr., Raymond A. *Life After Life*. Covington, GA:
Mockingbird Books, 1975.

Moody, Jr., Raymond A. *Reflections on Life After Life.* Covington, GA: Mockingbird Books, 1977.

Mundy, Jon. *Learning to Die.* Evanston, IL: Spiritual Frontiers Fellowship Publications, 1977.

Perkins, James S. *Through Death to Rebirth.* Wheaton, IL: Theosophical Publishing House, 1961.

Ring, Kenneth. "Religiousness and Near-Death Experiences: An Empirical Study." *Theta,* 8 (3), 1980.

_____. "The Experience of Dying." *Anabiosis,* 2 (2), 1980.

_____. *Life at Death.* New York: Coward, McCann & Geoghegan, 1980.

Sahler, Olle Jane Z. *The Child and Death.* St. Louis: C.U. Moslay Company, 1978.

Saraydarian, H. *The Science of Becoming Oneself.* Agoura, CA: The Aquarian Educational Group, 1969.

_____. *The Science of Meditation.* Agoura, CA: The Aquarian Educational Group, 1971.

Simonton, Carl and Stephanie Simonton. *Getting Well Again.* New York: Bantam Books, 1980.

Slater, Robert C. "Death From The Beginning." *Thanatos,* Vol. 5, 1979.

Stevenson, Ian. *Twenty Cases Suggestive of Reincarnation.* Charlottesville, VA: University Press of Virginia.

Stitt, Abby. "Emergency After Death." *Emergency Medicine,* March, 1971.

Weatherhead, Leslie D. *Life Begins at Death.* Nashville, TN: Abingdon, 1976.

I would like to share this information with others...

QUANTITY	BOOK TITLES	PRICE	TOTAL
	STEPPING STONES TO GRIEF RECOVERY —Deborah Roth	$8.95	
	GIFTS FOR THE LIVING: Conversations With Care-givers on Death and Dying —BettyClare Moffatt, et. al.	9.95	
	A NEW AGE HANDBOOK ON DEATH AND DYING —Carol Parrish-Harra	9.95	
	AIDS: A SELF-CARE MANUAL* —AIDS Project Los Angeles (320 pp.)	12.95	
	WHEN SOMEONE YOU LOVE HAS AIDS: A Book of Hope for Family & Friends —BettyClare Moffatt	8.95	
	SHIPPING & HANDLING ($2.00 for first book, $1.00 each additional book)		
	SALES TAX 6.5% (California residents only)		
	TOTAL DUE		

Please send check or money order to:

IBS PRESS
744 Pier Avenue
Santa Monica, CA 90405
(213) 450-6485

Name_____

Address_____

City/State/Zip_____

* Quantity discounts are available to AIDS-related organizations.